S0-BBT-850

At Issue

What Is the
Impact of Cyberlife?

Other Books in the At Issue Series:

At Issue

Montanto Family Library
D'Youville College

What Is the Impact of Cyberlife?

Andrea DeMott, Book Editor

GREENHAVEN PRESS
An imprint of Thomson Gale, a part of The Thomson Corporation

THOMSON

™

GALE

Detroit • New York • San Francisco • New Haven, Conn. • Waterville, Maine • London

Christine Nasso, *Publisher*
Elizabeth Des Chenes, *Managing Editor*

© 2008 The Gale Group.

Star logo is a trademark and Gale and Greenhaven Press are registered trademarks used herein under license.

For more information, contact:
Greenhaven Press
27500 Drake Rd.
Farmington Hills, MI 48331-3535
Or you can visit our Internet site at http://www.gale.com

ALL RIGHTS RESERVED
No part of this work covered by the copyright hereon may be reproduced or used in any form or by any means—graphic, electronic, or mechanical, including photocopying, record-ing, taping, Web distribution, or information storage retrieval systems—without the written permission of the publisher.

Articles in Greenhaven Press anthologies are often edited for length to meet page require-ments. In addition, original titles of these works are changed to clearly present the main thesis and to explicitly indicate the author's opinion. Every effort is made to ensure that Greenhaven Press accurately reflects the original intent of the authors. Every effort has been made to trace the owners of copyrighted material.

LIBRARY OF CONGRESS CATALOGING-IN-PUBLICATION DATA

What is the impact of cyberlife? / Andrea DeMott, book editor.
    p. cm. -- (At issue)
Includes bibliographical references and index.
ISBN-13: 978-0-7377-3876-6 (hardcover)
ISBN-13: 978-0-7377-3877-3 (pbk.)
  1. Information society. 2. Virtual reality. I. DeMott, Andrea B.
HM851.W44 2008
302.23'1--dc22
                                          2007034613

ISBN-10: 0-7377-3876-6 (hardcover)
ISBN-10: 0-7377-3877-4 (pbk.)

Printed in the United States of America
10 9 8 7 6 5 4 3 2 1

HM851
.W44
2008

Contents

AN 17 2008

Introduction

"The video game industry is entering a new era, an era where technology and creativity will fuse to produce some of the most stunning entertainment of the 21st Century. Decades from now, cultural historians will look back at this time and say it is when the definition of entertainment changed forever," Douglas Lowenstein, president of the Entertainment Software Association, said about a new generation of video games that has created a booming new industry.

Massively Multiplayer Online Role-Playing Games (MMORPGs) are accessed by many users at once through their personal computers over the Internet. The simulated environments in which these games take place are generally called virtual worlds, and according to Betsy Book on the Virtual Worlds Review Web site, they have several features in common. The "world" that the users share depicts space visually, ranging from two-dimensional "cartoon" imagery to more detailed three-dimensional environments, and the users usually participate by means of animated characters called "avatars." Virtual worlds are designed for interaction among the users; many of them encourage the formation of in-world social groups such as teams, guilds, or clubs. Virtual worlds are also persistent—that is, they continue to exist whether an individual user is logged in or not—and they are interactive, meaning that the users can alter, develop, or build upon the existing content. MMORPGs popular in early 2007 include Blizzard Entertainment's World of Warcraft and Sony Online Entertainment's EverQuest.

According to figures available on the MMOGChart.com Web site, in July 2006 the total number of people actively participating in these new games worldwide was close to thirteen million, although industry estimates often put that number much higher. The immense popularity is due to the "parents" that these MMORPGs share, R.V. Kelly suggests in *Massively Multiplayer Online Role-Playing Games: The People, the Addiction, and the Playing Experience.* In the popular role-playing game Dungeons & Dragons (D&D) from the 1970s, groups of players would meet together face-to-face, each one adopting a character—for example, a wizard, an elf, or a cleric—with predefined traits, abilities, and limitations. Within these roles, the players would act out an imaginary sword-and-sorcery adventure, using paper and pencil to track their progress. The 1970s also saw the introduction of Multi-User Dungeons (MUDs), text-only computerized adventures in imaginary castles and dungeons engaging several players at once using typed commands. In addition to containing narrative elements of the myths and legends of early civilizations, Kelly says, MMORPGs in the early 2000s "capture the feeling of direct action found in D&D. They connect players to an electronic world, as MUDs do. And, at the same time, they add the sound, movement, and fast pace of traditional blast-or-be-blasted console games. Maybe this combination of the most addictive features of other forms of storytelling and gaming is what makes MMORPGs so incredibly enticing."

The early precursors of MMORPGs could support up to sixteen users, but as the late 1990s brought increasing access to the Internet, computer processing power, and graphical capabilities of software, the numbers of simultaneous users that virtual worlds could support grew into the thousands, and the expression "massively multiplayer" was coined. Jack M. Balkin stated in "Virtual Liberty: Freedom to Design and Freedom to Play in Virtual Worlds": "As multiplayer game platforms become increasingly powerful and lifelike, they will be inevitably used for more than storytelling and entertainment. In the future, virtual worlds platforms will be adopted for commerce, for education, for professional, military, and vocational training, for medical consultation and psychotherapy . . . Although most virtual worlds today are currently an outgrowth of the gaming industry, they will become much more than that in time." The military, educational, and training uses for virtual worlds that Balkin predicted already exist in the early 2000s and have for some time. Popular new games such as Linden Lab's Second Life and Electronic Arts's The Sims Online are usually grouped under the less-restrictive title of MMOGs, since they lack role-playing elements; in these virtual worlds, users (via their avatars) do largely whatever they want. Many users participate for social or commercial reasons, rather than for entertainment, in the alternate realities provided by these games; thus their in-world activities can be called cyberlife rather than gaming.

In the August 2004 issue of *CyberPsychology & Behavior*, psychologist Mark Griffiths and his co-authors reported that the average age of players of one popular MMOG is 28 years old, 81 percent of the players are male, and the average time spent playing is close to 25 hours per week. The fact that people are flocking to MMOGs, and the fact that an ever-older segment of the population is spending more time immersed in their cyberlives than in their day jobs, is generating ever more attention and controversy. MMOGs are being blamed for a host of ills, including violence, addiction, promiscuity, and economic inequities. However, as an editorial in the August 6, 2005, edition of the *Economist* points out, skepticism of new media is an old tradition; the Internet itself was once condemned as a cesspool of depravity, but it is now recognized as a valuable new medium, although one where children's access should be limited and supervised. "As today's gamers grow older . . . video games will ultimately become just another medium, alongside books, music, and films. And soon the greying gamers will start tut-tutting about some new evil threatening to destroy the younger generation's moral fibre."

1

Virtual Worlds Are Becoming More Prevalent

Dave Gilson

Dave Gilson is research editor at Mother Jones *magazine. He has also written for the* San Francisco Chronicle, *the* East Bay Express, *and Salon.com.*

Facts and figures illustrate how popular and pervasive massively multiplayer online role-playing games have become. The population of these virtual worlds has become greater than that of a Central American capital. Many players spend more time inside the games than at their real jobs. The virtual economy of one online game could be larger than the economy of one real island country by the end of 2007.

The current population of virtual worlds, also known as "massively multiplayer online role-playing games" (MMORPGS) such as *World of Warcraft, EverQuest*, and *Second Life*, is estimated at more than 20 million. The population of Mexico City is 19 million.

20% of MMORPG gamers say that the virtual world is their primary place of residence. The real world, a.k.a. meatspace, is just a place to get food and sleep.

Virtual-world gamers play an average of 22 hours a week. The average American spends around 8 1/2 hours a week eating.

In 2005, the fantasy role-playing game *EverQuest* added a feature that allowed players to place a Pizza Hut order without leaving the keyboard.

Dave Gilson, "Even Better than the Real Thing," *Mother Jones*, May–June 2007, pp. 24–25. www.motherjones.com/news/exhibit/2007/05/exhibit.html. Copyright 2007 Foundation for National Progress. Reproduced by permission.

1/3 of *EverQuest* players spend more time inside the game than at their real jobs. 2 in 5 say that if they could make enough money inside the game they would quit their jobs.

Virtual Economics

MMORPG players say they spend an average of 135 real dollars buying virtual money.

EverQuest players spend an average of 23% more buying other players' male characters than female characters, even though both sexes have the same abilities in the game.

The virtual-currency trading company IGE Ltd. estimates that in 2007 players will spend $1.5 billion on virtual goods and services, from swords to sex.

The virtual-currency trading company IGE Ltd. estimates that in 2007 players will spend $1.5 billion on virtual goods and services, from swords to sex.

Entropia Universe offers its players a debit card that can be used at real-world ATMS to withdraw up to $3,000 a month from their supply of virtual cash.

In 2005, a man in China received a life sentence for murdering another gamer who had sold off his virtual sword inside the game *Legend of Mir 3*.

When a *World of Warcraft* player died last February, fellow gamers held an online memorial by a virtual lake "because she loved to fish in the game." The mourners, who came unarmed, were killed when the event was raided by rival players, who posted footage of the attack on YouTube.

84% of *World of Warcraft* players are male, and half of the game's female characters are created by men. Only 1% of male characters belong to women.

Second Life's economy was worth $86 million in 2006. At its current monthly growth rate of 15%, it could top $650 million this year. The GDP of Grenada is $578 million.

In January, Sweden announced it would be the first country to open an embassy inside *Second Life*. It is also considering taxing its citizens' virtual earnings.

Nearly half of online garners say they are addicted to their games.

An estimated 500,000 Chinese gamers are "gold farmers" who perform menial tasks inside online worlds to create virtual goods to sell to players in the West.

A typical gold farmer earns $65 to $100 a month.

Virtual Relationships

About 29% of female online gamers and 8% of male gamers say they've dated someone they first met in a game.

1/3 of female gamers make their characters get married; 10% of male players do. A *Second Life* minister who performs avatar weddings says most virtual marriages last about a month.

A survey of college-aged *Sims* players found that 50% with divorced parents made their game characters get divorced. No players whose parents were still married did.

When a Chinese couple filed for divorce in 2005, the husband reportedly tried to keep $5,000 worth of virtual property in exchange for their real-world apartment. The wife wanted to split both. They had met the year before inside an online game.

The editor of *Slustler*, a magazine with explicit images of *Second Life* avatars, says, "The 'girl next door' effect is way higher than in real porn. . . . You could actually meet the people you see in the magazine."

An hour with a virtual escort in *Second Life* costs between 4 and 12 real dollars.

"*O Mee Pooba*" means "I'm pregnant" in "Simlish," the language spoken in *The Sims*.

The Bare Naked Ladies, the Black Eyed Peas, and Depeche Mode have recorded songs in Simlish.

Celebrities who have appeared as avatars in *Second Life* include Jay-Z, Arianna Huffington, former Virginia governor Mark Warner, Suzanne Vega, and Kurt Vonnegut.

Virtual Battle

Formed to fight for political rights for avatars, the Second Life Liberation Army has bombed a virtual Reebok store and shot avatars shopping at American Apparel.

For $1,500, live-shot.com offered armchair hunters the chance to shoot a real animal via the Internet. After lining up crosshairs on their computer screen, visitors could fire live rounds with a click of the mouse.

In 2003, [the Middle Eastern paramilitary organization] Hezbollah released a video game in which players were awarded medals for throwing grenades at images of Ariel Sharon.

America's Army, the Army's recruitment video game, has been downloaded 17 million times. "It shows we are not robots," explained an Iraq vet who appears as a character in the game. "We're just people."

The Navy has spent $4 million to study the use of virtual reality to treat PTSD [Post-Traumatic Stress Disorder]. Says an official, "We also hope that this type of therapy, with its video-game-like qualities, will resonate well with the current generation of warfighters."

Nearly half of online gamers say they are addicted to their games.

"Gamesterdam," a rehab program for video-game addicts, opened in Holland last July [2006] to "give these people a taste of life. Real life!"

2

The Popularity of Virtual Worlds Is Exaggerated

Cade Metz

New Jersey-based Cade Metz, senior writer at PC Magazine, *writes about growth and change in the technology landscape.*

Businesses are taking virtual worlds such as Second Life *very seriously. Major companies are building virtual "campuses," three-dimensional Web sites where they can advertise their products—or sell them. Along with the media, these companies are eager to tell the public how popular* Second Life *is, although in truth, no one knows how many potential customers are actually using the game or whether it makes sense as a marketing tool. If players resent big-name companies intruding on their virtual creations, or if people prefer telephone calls over virtual-world chat, as a virtual home for real-world businesses,* Second Life *may remain little more than a curiosity.*

On December 1 [2006], Ross Mayfield held a press conference inside World of Warcraft. In real life, Mayfield is the CEO of SocialText, a Palo Alto start-up offering online collaboration software for enterprise-scale businesses. In World of Warcraft, a 3D game that serves as a kind of alternate online universe, he's a sword-wielding knight named Kalevipoeg. More than 30 bloggers and reporters attended the press conference, using their own sword-wielding avatars, and no one was allowed to ask Mayfield a question without challenging his virtual knight to a virtual duel.

Cade Metz, "The Emperor's New Web," *PC Magazine*, vol. 26, no. 9, April 24, 2007, pp. 70–77. Copyright © 2007 Ziff Davis Publishing Holdings Inc. All rights reserved. Reproduced by permission.

When Mayfield first announced this online Q&A session, via his personal blog, it was no more than a joke. He was poking fun at companies like Dell and Sun, which had recently held press conferences inside Second Life, the online virtual world that has an awful lot in common with World of Warcraft. Much to his surprise, readers took him seriously, and more than a few asked if they could join in. So he went ahead with his World of Warcraft press conference, and the press actually came, including a mainstream business reporter who soon published a story in the Austin *American-Statesman*.

To the surprise of many, the business world—that's the real business world—has fallen head over heels for Second Life and other virtual worlds. Last May, *BusinessWeek* ran a Second Life cover story. In October, Reuters opened a virtual news bureau inside the service that had veteran tech journalist Adam Pasick trolling for stories with help from a digital alter ego. And shortly thereafter, as some were beginning to wonder whether the service was overhyped, *Fortune* senior editor David Kirkpatrick ran a story called "No, Second Life Is Not Overhyped."

Virtual worlds may indeed play a big role in the future of the Internet. But for the moment, the talk far exceeds the actual worth of these services—at least in business terms.

Real Business Enchantment with the Virtual World

Companies like Dell and Sun aren't just holding press conferences inside this alternative universe. They're building virtual "campuses," 3D Web sites where they can advertise their products—or even sell them. Cisco holds interactive seminars inside Second Life, complete with video feeds of featured speakers, while IBM uses the service for internal communication, with far-flung employees chatting away via digital avatars. The company claims that more than 3,000 IBMers have participated in these virtual-world chats, including everyone from marketing types to software developers.

"We're at the beginning of the next evolution of the Internet—the 3D Internet, as we like to call it," says IBM's Michael Rowe, whose official title is senior manager, 3D Internet and Virtual Worlds. "If Web 2.0 is a place where everyone becomes a producer, everyone becomes a content creator, the 3D Internet gives us a whole new level of social interaction in this collaborative space."

But the question remains: Is Second Life overhyped? If you talk to companies that have set up shop in this virtual world—or if you read about Second Life in the press—you're inevitably told how popular it is. "It's hugely popular," says Rowe. "The growth curve is enormous." More often than not, you'll hear that Second Life boasts *millions* of users. But the truth of the matter is that no one knows how many people are using the service—other than Linden Labs, the company that hosts Second Life. According to Clay Shirky, a faculty member in the Interactive Telecommunications Program at NYU who's made a four-month study of Second Life's audience, the number of regular users is well under 200,000.

Virtual worlds may indeed play a big role in the future of the Internet. But for the moment, the talk far exceeds the actual worth of these services—at least in business terms. If fewer than 200,000 people are regularly using Second Life, it's not the best marketing tool. And though virtual worlds are certainly a means of long-distance communication, it's yet to be seen whether this makes sense—in the long term—for anything other than fun and games.

So many companies are entering Second Life because it's the thing to do, because the press gives virtual worlds so much attention. "The biggest benefit of Second Life—for companies—is the media attention," says Heather McConnell, an account executive with the international PR firm Hill &

Knowlton, who's become the in-house virtual worlds expert, educating clients on these new age services. "The media is generating so many stories about companies entering Second Life, and that's a real advantage." But this sort of press coverage lasts for only so long. In the end, virtual worlds aren't viable business tools unless they offer something more, and whatever the claims of Cisco, IBM, or *Fortune*, it's hard to tell if they actually will.

Certainly some people are visiting these in-world business campuses. But without reliable, third-party traffic-monitoring software, it's hard to tell exactly how many.

The Massively Multiplayer Online Commerce Engine

There's a reason Ross Mayfield equates Second Life with World of Warcraft. It looks and feels very much like an online 3D game. Thousands of users navigate the same sprawling digital universe using cartoon-like avatars. *BusinessWeek*'s seminal Second Life cover story, "My Virtual Life," actually calls it a "massively multiplayer online game," comparing it directly with World of Warcraft.

But unlike 3D games, Second Life isn't about winning. There are no goals or levels. It's a place where you live, yes, a second life. You don't sword-fight or blow things up—unless you want to. You walk around. You chat with people. You go dancing, skiing, scuba diving, or shopping. Second Life has its own economy, based on virtual "Linden dollars," letting you buy and sell virtual goods—from shirts, shoes, and trinkets to cars, houses, and real estate. There's an open market where you can trade real American money for Linden dollars, but as you buy and sell goods "in-world," you can also find ways of generating virtual currency from scratch.

The trick is that, in Second Life, you're free to create your own virtual objects. There's a limited amount of virtual land, but with Linden Labs supplying the modeling tools, you can build almost anything else. And whatever you create, you own—even in the real world. Intellectual property rights belong to the builder. Once you build an object, you can keep it for yourself or sell it to someone else. That means you have free rein to personalize your digital avatar or your own digital home, but you can also open your own digital boutique, selling anything from handbags to hairdos.

Many die-hard users are unhappy about big brand name joining the fun. And . . . because users can do almost anything short of destruction, business operations are easily disrupted.

Second Life gives users a certain amount of control they may not have in the real world. You can be someone you're not. And if you're shrewd enough, you might even make some serious money. A woman named Ailin Graef, whose avatar appeared on the cover of *BusinessWeek*, claims that her virtual bank account and virtual real estate holdings make her a real-world millionaire.

At the same time, this create-buy-and-sell dynamic gives entrée to real-world businesses. Adidas, for instance, can promote its shoe brand by building a virtual store where it sells virtual shoes. Think of this as a kind of 3D Web site, a cartoon-like retail outlet where avatars can come and shop. Meanwhile, Dell can open an in-world island where it sells *real PCs*, as it does at Dell.com. Cisco and IBM can fashion digital campuses where distant employees, clients, partners, and even customers can communicate. All of this is happening today. But you have to wonder if any of it actually makes sense.

My Virtual Business Is Virtually Empty

In December, Greg Verdino, the vice president of emerging channels at the tech-savvy marketing firm Digitas, took a tour of Second Life's big-name business campuses, including Starwood's virtual hotel, the Aloft, and virtual stores from American Apparel, Toyota, and Reebok. None of them contained even a single customer.

Certainly, some people are visiting these in-world business campuses. But without reliable third-party traffic-monitoring software, it's hard to tell exactly how many. Cisco monitors its traffic tools from a site called SL Stats.com, but these aren't widely used. Because Second Lifers can so easily create dummy avatars, even Linden Labs concedes that such tools are less than reliable. "It's easy to create an object that sits on a virtual parcel and looks for avatars," says Daniel Huebner, Second Life's community director. "But we're beginning to see 'bots' in Second Life. It's possible that there are avatars in the world that are not backed by human beings."

There may come a time when virtual worlds are a legitimate means of marketing and selling products. The 3D imagery could give people a better idea of what real products actually look like. Some even argue that virtual worlds will bring a certain social element to online stores, letting you discuss products with the people shopping beside you. This sort of retail chat doesn't happen much in the real world, but if anything, the past 15 years have shown that many people are more comfortable chatting with strangers over the Web than they are in the flesh.

"Existing businesses trying to make an extra buck in Second Life? Probably won't pan out. . . . The bottom line is that Second Life is just a chat-room video game."

Of course, you can always augment a 2D Web site with 3D imagery, and at this point, you can't be sure that people actually enjoy browsing products with a digital avatar. A site like Amazon.com is successful because it makes shopping so easy, and in many ways, virtual worlds make shopping more complicated. Virtual marketing may seem like a much simpler animal—all you have to do is get your company name in front of that wandering avatar—but its effectiveness is even harder to judge. At least until these technologies mature.

"Can you, as a business, look at the Second Life of today and say it's a viable marketing channel? Can you draw direct lines between what people do in Second Life and what they do in real life?" Verdino asks. "No, you can't. Certainly, Second Life is innovative, but it's far too early to start calculating ROI, or expect any real-world deliverables to come of it."

The War on Virtual Terror

Two months after Verdino's stroll through some very empty Second Life campuses, a group calling itself the Second Life Liberation Army detonated two virtual bombs outside the American Apparel and Reebok stores. Angry that businesses and other elite users are buying up the prime Second Life real estate and exerting an undue amount of power over the service, the group is calling for Linden Labs to cede political rights to each and every member.

This didn't "damage" the virtual stores. You can't destroy other users' property without hacking the service. But it points to a pair of problems facing any business that enters Second Life. For one, many die-hard users are unhappy about the big brand names joining the fun. And, two, because users can do almost anything short of destruction, business operations are easily disrupted—sometimes intentionally, sometimes not. This fall, an innocent bystander disrupted Toyota's virtual Scion unveiling when he accidentally drove his car onto the stage.

Linden Labs reserves the right to remove misbehaving users from the service, but that's the only protection businesses have against in-world disruptions—short of real-world lawsuits, and this sort of thing has yet to be tested. "If you're going to create a virtual world, with a virtual economy and virtual people, you're going to need a virtual dispute mechanism—and there's not one," says Alan Behr, a partner in the electronic entertainment group at Alston & Bird, an East Coast law firm.

Yes, you can hold private gatherings in Second Life. When IBM uses the service for internal communication, uninvited guests are prevented from participating by privacy tools built into the service. But exclusion doesn't make sense with sales and marketing, and circumventing privacy tools isn't difficult. At this point, Second Life has no reliable security mechanism, either.

Conference Calls Reloaded

Over the next year, IBM will spend $10 million on virtual-world technologies. That's real American currency. Big Blue is helping other businesses build virtual campuses—Circuit City and Sears stores are already open inside Second Life—but a big part of its push involves that notion of 3D business communication. Rowe of IBM believes that in-world chats are more natural and more "fun" than everyday telephone conference calls.

"When a traditional conference call ends, everyone hangs up and they go back to work," Rowe says. "In Second Life, even with the global reach of our company and all the different time zones and cultures, people stick around at the end and socialize. They'll strike up conversations that are natural in a physical setting but that don't really happen on a conference call. There's a real collaborative feeling to it. It's a powerful thing for a business to have."

Or a huge time sink. In some ways, virtual-world chat is just a more cumbersome and time-consuming version of instant messaging, and although Web-based video conferencing has been around for years, offering a visual experience that's in some ways superior to 3D chat, most people still prefer good old-fashioned telephone calls.

R. David Lankes, an associate professor at Syracuse University's School of Information Studies, sees virtual-world communication as no more than a novelty. "I set up an office in Second Life—and I was addicted for a whole week," he says. "I taught a class in Second Life, and at one point I realized we were just chatting. We could do that over IM."

Now You See It, Now You Don't

No doubt, there's a social component to virtual worlds you won't find with other technologies. But many wonder whether this transfers to the business world. As much as the mainstream press writes about Second Life, few reporters point out that one of the most popular activities is sex. HUGSaLOT, a Second Life escort who asks that her real-world identity be kept secret, claims that her virtual world activities earn upward of 500 American dollars a month.

As someone who's used the service for more than two years, she concedes that some real-world businesses will thrive in Second Life, but she's sure that most of them will flop. "Existing businesses trying to make an extra buck in Second Life? Probably won't pan out. They won't be accepted," she says. "The bottom line is that Second Life is just a chat-room video game."

But the so-called 3D Internet doesn't exist. Second Life is just one Web service with a relatively small number of regular users. You can point to the millions of people using World of Warcraft—and actually paying for the privilege—but World of Warcraft is by no means a business tool. As massively multiplayer online games go, Second Life is just different enough to provide a virtual home for real-world businesses, but at the moment, the role of these companies is little more than a curiosity.

Then again, maybe the 3D Internet does exist. Maybe it's here because so many people believe that it's here. Maybe it's the future of the Web because no one wants to admit that it's not. If you hold a press conference in World of Warcraft and the press actually comes, is it still a joke?

3

Virtual Worlds Pointlessly Imitate Real Life

Jenny Diski

Jenny Diski, a British writer and author of eight novels, is a regular contributor to the Observer *of London and the* London Review of Books.

The online role-playing game Second Life *attracts over a million simulated inhabitants whose only task is to create anything they want. A visit to* Second Life *reveals, however, that it is controlled by the same ordinary beings as the real one: players engage in buying and selling, profit and consumption, material decoration and political apathy, just like they do in real life. Second Life is touted as the virtual world where this world can be done better, but its players just seem to be creating this same sad little world all over again.*

Most religions suggest that we get at least one other go at being. Christianity offers an after-life, Judaism suggests an altogether better existence once the Messiah arrives, while Hinduism and other Eastern religions try to deal with samsara, the terrible burden of having to do life over and over again until you get it right. But I don't think any of them offer much help with the alarming notion of multiple worlds, which quantum theorists have arithmeticked to prove entirely possible. As far as I can understand it, Many Worlds Theory proposes that there are *n* zillion worlds like this one but mar-

Jenny Diski, "Jowls Are Available," *London Review of Books*, vol. 29, February 8, 2007, pp. 14–15. www.lrb.co.uk/v29/n03/disk01_.html. Appears here by permission of the London Review of Books.

ginally different, operating in parallel to the only world in which we think we exist. There you're wearing pink kitten heels not Hush Puppies, there you had sausage for breakfast not muesli, there it so happened that you took a left turn not a right one and became a fashionistic, carnivoracious arch-criminal instead of the peace-negotiating, vegan, style waste-land you are in this world. We might each be living out all our possible lives, through all the variations of what we could possibly say or do, in an infinite number of worlds where everyone else is living out their variations, each at some weird angle to this one that my sorry, innumerate and spatially challenged brain is unable to comprehend. If this sounds like hell on earths to you then you probably haven't signed up for *Second Life*.

Second Life is a virtual online world that exists on a vast computer somewhere in California. It has a detailed landscape, a mainland, many islands and more than one million simulated inhabitants whose actual bodies are distributed around every part of the physical world. It's called a game though there is no goal and no end point at which a clear winner emerges and takes the prize. In this it is no different from real life (RL, as it's referred to in SL). And it's free up to a point, which is the entrance price of real life, though just like the here and now, if you want to own any part of the world in *Second Life*, you need money to buy it. There are of course differences between RL and SL. You have to opt in to SL, which is a degree of volition you don't get in reality. This does give it a certain negative charm: at least there is one possible life to which you can just say no. It also has the edge on the real thing (for me, at least, as an über-indolent person), because being a virtual world, you don't have to go out to get to it. I used to weep envious buckets watching whatshisname in *Close Encounters of the Third Kind* being taken off-world to the absolutely not here anymore by those delightful doe-eyed creatures, and *Second Life* seemed to offer a way of doing this without the hassle of the striving, making mountains out of mashed potato, quest thing. So I signed up.

It turns out that there is no second life on Second Life, *only more of the same old first and only one, but cartoon-shaped.*

The problem turned out to be (as it must) that *Second Life* is organised and inhabited by beings from the real world who have by definition very little experience of being anywhere or any way else. Being virtual is not very different from being real because the virtual place and its beings are controlled by the same old us as always. I heard the Tory politician Bill Cash on the radio the other day explaining that we needed to repeal the Human Rights Act because it was formulated and operated by idealists. I suppose it was my idealist tendencies which caused my difficulty with *Second Life*. I shouldn't have been surprised, but was, that this alternative world has a material life and economy uncannily similar to the one we're already stuck with. If you are looking for another way of being, you'll be deeply disappointed. But you probably won't be because you will understand that it couldn't be otherwise. I was beguiled by the idea of a world apart from the real world which people keep telling me I have to come to terms with. It turns out that there is no second life on *Second Life*, only more of the same old first and only one, but cartoon-shaped. In *Second Life* each individual can take little bits of processing power, learn to manipulate them and make two-dimensional objects of any kind. Linden Lab, the owners of *Second Life*, guarantee that everyone will retain the real world intellectual property rights to their virtual creations. So is the place stuffed full of extraordinary experimental poetry, song, fiction, art and architecture?

Second Life is a reiteration. It's a virtual world of buying and selling, profit and consumption, material decoration and political apathy. What you get in this alternative world are houses, home decorations, clothes, jewelery, cars, motorbikes, casinos, strip clubs and shops in which to sell all these things to cartoon characters representing their computer owners, who 'live' in the houses on the virtual land they have bought, titivate their interiors, change their clothes, hair and jewellery, drive the cars, gamble in the casinos and stand around gazing at naked pole dancers. That is to say, staring at cartoons who shimmy up to two-dimensional poles and rub their pixillated breasts and pudenda in the time-honoured weary wanton manner. There is education. Tutors explain how to manipulate the pixels to make things, and there are American colleges running courses for their paying students. Of Socrates in the agora there is no sign.

Inventing the Avatar

You join *Second Life* in the form of an 'avatar'. The first—and most entertaining—thing you do when you arrive is invent yourself. Beginning with a basic set of templates (hot chick, hunk, businesswoman, sporty type), you tweak dozens of detailed physical elements until you get something you want. Skin, eye and hair colour, clothing and height are all under your control. The inner and outer corners of your eyes can be turned incrementally up and down, your lips made fuller or thinner, ditto thighs, waist and pecs; cheekbones can be more or less prominent and higher or lower, ditto forehead, nose and breasts. Eventually, your avatar becomes a caricature of what you have always wanted to be, exactly what you are, or in some cases a large furry animal. In fact, by far the majority of the avatars are of the first kind. Offered the possibility of designing their own physiognomy, it seems very few people can resist producing the tinseltown dream version. *Second Life* is almost entirely inhabited by impossibly long-legged, big-breasted, muscle-rippling blondes with lips so plumped full of what would be collagen in the real world that they make Ivana

Trump's mouth look mean. The males are much the same, only taller. What this place needs is a grumpy old woman, I thought, and decided to become *Second Life*'s single example of an older generation. I made my avatar into a woman of 60, with wrinkles and jowls (they are available), downturned mouth and eyes, white hair, shapeless black jeans and a black sweater, and set off to find the nearest marketplace to mutter all kinds of thin-lipped warnings to the frivoling young. . . .

My fantasy self couldn't actually read my unreal book because an avatar doesn't read or do anything, being entirely dependent on the will and brainpower of a real self out here in First Life directing it.

After a while I gave up wandering the earth (flying and teleporting in fact) with my messages of cultural dismay, and started asking questions of the helpful employees of Linden Labs made virtual flesh and available to assist the bewildered novice. (Speech is keyed in and appears on the screen in a small box. It's slow.) They invariably answered my question 'What is there to do here?' with: 'Well, what do you like to do in RL? You can meet people, dance, gamble, date, buy clothes, hang out . . . whatever you want.'

In fact, I only like to do two of those things, and gambling I do anyway in cyberspace, while clothes only please me when they are actually hanging in my cupboard or on my body.

'But why wouldn't I do the things I like in the real world in the real world?'

'Because here you can do them better.'

I was taken with the notion of becoming a great painter, but I couldn't see how *Second Life* would make me great at what I'm no good at in real life. If I wanted to think of myself as a great painter in spite of what I made on canvas or screen, I could just as well be delusional in the here and now. The point of a virtual existence became less and less clear to me.

'I watch TV, read, and I listen to music.'

Virtual Things to Do

TV wasn't an option in *Second Life* unless staring at a screen, talking at two-dimensional figures who are not what they pretend to be counts. Virtual concerts are available. The Arctic Monkeys (I think) had bought an island and were doing gigs on it, but no Beethoven quartets or Tom Waits concerts were listed when I searched for them. In any case, my computer doesn't have the kind of sound system that would make even the Arctic Monkeys sound as they should. For reading, I was directed to the Library, where, this being a simulacrum of the modern world, for a few Linden dollars I bought a copy of Shakespeare's *Sonnets*. But reading, after all, is and always has been a second life. So now a virtual me was carrying around a virtual book of poetry. And if my avatar (Jehu, I called my/herself) could have read it I/she would have done so to keep the virtual world out, just as I have done for much of my real life. Though, of course, my fantasy self couldn't actually read my unreal book because an avatar doesn't read or do anything, being entirely dependent on the will and brainpower of a real self out here in First Life directing it.

I had hopes of there being some kind of politics in *Second Life*. Maybe there were cyber-revolutionaries intent on subverting the pointless mimicry of the real world or an underground working to overturn the autocratic rule of the Lindens. . . .

When 15 members of the Front National lately acquired land and built their headquarters on *Second Life* things did take something of a political turn. Anti-fascist avatars turned up and demonstrated. A battle ensued. Political rage, *Second Life* style, is expressed by chucking exploding pink pigs at your opponents, strafing them with virtual machine guns, pelting them with holograms of marijuana leaves or anything else you fancy making with your little bits of processing power.

The Le Pen brigade built another HQ in a different part of town, its walls covered with heroic studies of their leader. Supporters mill about inside and outside the building wearing muscles and white T-shirts. When I flew in to take a look, there was a brief demonstration by invisible forces who bombarded the area with fluttery anti-Front National signs and flying placards picturing a Hitler-moustached Le Pen. How strange to have an extreme nationalist party setting up shop in a hallucinated, incorporeal world. But excellent publicity for Linden Lab.

And sex? Nearby advertising hoardings suggested that anyone wanting to earn some easy Linden dollars should apply for work at the Sexy Vixens' Play Den. There is a red-light district in *Second Life*. I arrived in Amsterdam (why be original in the unoriginal world of sexual fantasy?) and found crowds of male and female avatars hanging about outside booths where erotic dancers enticed customers into the club. A notice outside the Sexy Vixens' Play Den warned against competitors. . . .

On the street, female avatars dressed in thigh boots, glittering bustiers or naked but for a thong and high heels, offered pussy in return for between L$500 and L$700. . . .

It's less a case of do it better than do it again: in fact, this seems to be its chief attraction.

'What do you do apart from talk dirty?'

'Everything. Anything you like in RL I can do for you here. And you can do things here you've only dreamed about.'

I had a complete failure of imagination.

'How?'

'Give me some money and I'll show you.'

I know this sounds like 'I made my excuses and left,' but part of me was very sorry that, after paying for the Sonnets, I had just L$244 left of the L$250 the nice people at Linden

Labs give everyone to get started. It wasn't a large enough part, however, to justify submitting to this paper's publisher an expenses claim for virtual sexual enlightenment.

A Replication of the Regular World

Aside from the mystery of the poseballs and the sex gun beds, nothing else about *Second Life* suggested a novel way of being. I suppose that I misread the whole thing. 'Second' doesn't mean 'alternative'. But not only does *Second Life* not offer an alternative existence, it positively encourages a replication of the regular world. It's less a case of do it better than do it again: in fact, this seems to be its chief attraction. There is an embedded Reuters correspondent in *Second Life* working from a virtual Reuters building and reporting both in-world and in reality. In the foyer I met a reporter from al-Jazeera trying, like me, to figure out what the point was. So far he hadn't come up with one. One recent excitement in the actual world's press was caused by the discovery that people were making real and quite serious money by doing just what people do in RL: buying and selling, accumulating surplus, exploiting scarcity, creating desire, selling their labour, begging. You can buy and sell the Linden dollar on real world currency exchanges. It fluctuates, but currently L$247.5 is worth US$1. Land is created and controlled by Linden Labs. It represents computer power and they lease it out to purchasers for a monthly fee plus a US$9.95 monthly upgrade on the free account which secures the right to buy. Land can be sold, sublet and built on. One early land-grabber made US$200,000 in real life last year [in 2006] by speculating on *Second Life* property. Another virtual world based in the Netherlands, *Entropy Universe*, has made the economic link between fantasy and reality even stronger by building degeneration into everything that exists on it. Not just clothes and cars wear out, but presumably bodies, too. And no silly sentimentality about a national health service to worry about. A virtual money-market currency and built-in obsolescence is a perfect world indeed.

It makes the old Gnostic version of the Creation, which has a junior deity creating our universe to practise on, look compellingly plausible. The senior gods have surely long since produced a much nicer immaterial universe in which we, half-arsed underling attempt at a world that we are, cannot participate. And being what we are, and techno-whizzes to boot, we can and do perpetually reproduce our own conditions in increasingly sophisticated formats. A very different kind of multiple world theory, where the same sad little world is made over and over again. I really hope that our alternative selves, in at least some of those infinite parallel worlds the quantum physicists tell of, are doing better.

4

Personal Interaction Is a Valued Component of Online Games

T. L. Taylor

T. L. Taylor is associate professor in the Department of Digital Aesthetics and Communication at the IT University of Copenhagen, Denmark.

Online games often inspire the assumption that gaming is an isolating and alienating activity indulged in by solitary teenage boys. But online games are fundamentally social spaces. Players tend to draw their family members into the games, and the pre-existing connections between players offline help them advance in the game. In-game connections that players move offline are also very important parts of the games' impact on society, as is the network of offline meetings, information sources, and creative works that develop from the game.

Over the years I have heard repeatedly of people coming to EQ [EverQuest] because of a family member, friend, or coworker. Kim, for example, met her husband in the game (something she does not tell too many people, given the stigma often attached) and now their family plays together. As she put it, "Four people, four computers, one server." Another woman, Katinka, who became a regular part of my game life and was in several guilds with me over the course of the years, began the game because her husband (who had himself been

T. L. Taylor, *Play Between Worlds: Exploring Online Game Culture*, Cambridge, MA: MIT Press, 2006. © 2006 T. L. Taylor. All rights reserved. Reproduced by permission of The MIT Press, Cambridge, MA.

playing for a while with his friends) sat down one night and made her a character based on one of her tried-and-true *D&D* [Dungeons and Dragons] characters. In the course of my research, it was not at all uncommon to find that people were connected to other players through a variety of preexisting offline ties. Indeed, in the case of women and power gamers . . . this is particularly notable. Besides providing an explanation for how people first are exposed to the game, however, offline ties between players also serve as an important component in the enjoyment of the game.

The Importance of Offline Connections

In the following example, I am having a conversation with a young guildmember, Dargon, that turns to the subject of family.

Dargon: I only wanted to have an alt for awhile he is a STD

TL: A what darg?

Dargon: A STD super twinked dwarf

TL: Heh, ah.

Dargon: My uncle said i was that and i got laughed at by him so i stop[p]ed his moeny [sic] source for awhile

TL: Lol

TL: How many in your family play darg?

Dargon: I think 7 or 8

TL: Wow, nice

TL: Did you guys get them into it or them you?

Dargon: Both uncles on dads side sister brother and me dad and then 2 cousins

Dargon: We got my 1 of my uncles but the other got it for his B day by his wife (who now regrets it)

TL: Aw, heh. do you guys group together a lot?

Dargon: And the cousins we got them into it *TL smiles.*

Dargon: Well the one we got in to it he is lvl 9 chanter so my 10 dwarf can and the my other uncle has about a million characters on in the guild even i group with him a lot and my cousins i group with a lot but the group is different i PL [power level] them

TL: Ah, gotcha, still pretty cool, didn't realize you had all kinds of family in [the guild]. heh, neat:)

Dargon: We have are only little chat thing set up to wear we get on and join the chat

TL: Oh, handy:)

It is not at all unusual to find players helping newbies they know offline by giving them some money, items, or, just as important, crucial game advice and tips.

Here we see the way an extended family negotiates the game space. It is not unlike the stories you hear from many other players in which a kind of domino effect occurs whereby yet one more family member finds themselves picking up the game and starting her own character. One interesting aspect of this particular example is the elevated position Dargon has inside the game. When his uncle teases him about his character, he retaliates by freezing in-game monetary support. Dargon has a kind of duality to his status within the family. On the one hand because he is young he often is not in the same position of power as his parents, aunts and uncles, or cousins. But in-game this dynamic is flipped and he has opportunities to occupy the more powerful or higher status position. James

Gorman, in his piece in the *New York Times* entitled "The Family That Slays Demons Together," recounts a similar experience in which he found himself relying on the help—both knowledge and financial—of his son in the game *Diablo II*. He writes of one of their in-game shopping excursions:

> "This one I'll buy for you," he [his son] said, pointing out the Plated Belt of Thorns (which I now wear), "but if you go for the more expensive one, you'll have to pay yourself." I could hear my own voice, in the aisles of Toys "R" Us, urging moderation in the purchase of Beast War transformers.

It is important to note that game relationships quite often move offline and that players regularly form out-of-game relationships with each other.

Families and Friends as Social Capital

These situations also point to the ways families and friends bring social capital into the game space through preexisting relationships. While it is sometimes called twinking, it is not at all unusual to find players helping newbies they know offline by giving them some money, items, or, just as important, crucial game advice and tips. Beyond game objects and knowledge, out-of-game relationships give players an instant social network in the game. Cousins can introduce a new player around, coworkers can put together groups to help the new player, and in general the existing in-game networks can be marshaled to help the new player. These offline connections also provide unique situations in which people sometimes play together in the same shared physical space, where the benefits of instant easy communication or handing off keyboards, if needed, are also apparent.

While I have so far suggested that offline connections are primarily ones that predate the players' entry into the game, it is important to note that game relationships quite often move offline and that players regularly form out-of-game relationships with each other. This is something we see in other Internet spaces, as well, so it should come as no real surprise that people who form regular meaningful relationships in the game space might want to pursue them offline. This can occur in a range of different ways.

Katinka—I previously mentioned that her husband created the original character for her—was only one member of a very close extended family-and-friends group that I spent much time with over the years. In fact, I first met her through her husband, Jack, who played in the game. Both being Gnomes, we found a kind of instant playful bond that many Gnomes seem to have in the game. As I spent more time with the couple, I came to see that they negotiated a very interesting set of relationships. Quite often they were in separate guilds (though regularly with secondary characters in a common one) and had an extended friendship network that piggybacked on many other offline relationships. Katinka's cousin, for example, was a player I also ran into with some regularity, and Katinka played with a group made up primarily of husbands, wives, cousins, and close in-game friends. . . .

Several times I spent evenings with sets of couples who shared character last names but were, I would find out in back-channel, actually married offline to other players.

In-Game Marriages

One of the most interesting things I saw in my time with this group was the ways partners often negotiated semi-role-played extramarital game relationships and friendship bonds. Once a character reaches level 20 in *EQ* the player is allowed to give it a last name. Several times I spent evenings with sets of couples who shared character last names but were, I would find out in back-channel, actually married offline to other players. Katinka, for example, shared a last name with Vin, one of the other members of our guild who was not her husband. She and Vin had developed a fairly close friendship over the years and while the last name signified an in-game marriage (of several years), it was as much a marker of a deep friendship commitment. After several years they decided to meet and Vin flew from his home in Hawaii to visit Katinka and her husband (who he also knew from in the game) at their home in Texas.

TL: How was that, meeting him for the first time?

Katinka: Oh, God, I was a nervous wreck. I'm gonna meet my best OOC [out of character] friend in real life. I hadn't slept in 24 hours. Do you remember Rianna?

TL: Yeah, I do.

Katinka: Well she's my cousin. She was staying with me that night. She was going to go to the airport with me, because I can't find my way out of a wet paper sack without a map, a flashlight, and a Sherpa to guide me. It's like 7 in the morning, we haven't slept, because I'm rushing around the house trying to make sure everything's just right. We get to the airport, we're sitting there, and we're completely loony by this time, so we're sitting there waiting for his plane to come in. I don't have the slightest idea what he looks like really, I've seen one picture of him. He told me what he was going to be wearing, so we gotta look for this guy wearing this. And all of a sudden all these little A- cause he's Asian, all of a sudden all these Asians get off the plane and I'm like "Oh, my God," and I'm looking for him and there he is, so I'm like "okay." So we get him and we give him a hug and we could have knocked each other over because neither one of us had slept. So, it was great, ya know, being able to meet him.

TL: Was he different than you expected him to be?

Katinka: If he had been any quieter he would have been dead. He's not a very loud person. And being from Texas, ya know, we are just loud—you don't take us out in public if you can avoid it. He's a lot like how he is in the game, just quieter. And after the first day or two we were able to relax and act completely silly.

TL: And was that your first time meeting somebody that you had only met online?

Katinka: Yeah.

TL: Interesting. Would you do it again, do you think?

Katinka: Yeah, I think so.

TL: And did it end up changing how you guys were able to interact with each other online?

Katinka: Not really, because we got to be really great friends before we met, and we're still really good friends now. It wasn't very different.

This ability to have relationships that might not otherwise occur without the game strikes me as one of the fundamental ways spaces like MMOGs are reorganizing social life. As children and teens occupy positions of power, as inter-generational friendships develop, as partners find new friendship networks not solely reliant on a nuclear family, as people develop deep connections with those who live far from them or whom they never meet in person, these game spaces offer interesting possibilities to undo some of the constraint produced by traditional families and localized friendship pools.

5

Sex Is Integral to Virtual Worlds

Mitch Wagner

Mitch Wagner is senior online news editor for Information-Week, *a weekly magazine for business technology professionals. He has also worked as a reporter and editor at several other publications in the computer trade press.*

The world of online games is a haven where people can fulfill their sexual fantasies. Second Life *residents engage in cybersex for a variety of reasons, from making a profit to having fun to healing from prior sexual abuse. Cybersex involving adults playing the role of children inspires controversy, though, and allegations of child molestation and pornography have led to a government investigation. While the company behind* Second Life *is working to limit or eliminate such activities, company executives maintain that cybersex is healthy. Although it can be viewed as the product of an anonymous environment free of consequences, sex in the virtual world is really driven by deep emotional relationships.*

The hype is familiar by now: You can do anything in *Second Life*: Go parachuting, go surfing, build a majestic building, fight vampires.

Or you can have sex.

As with every medium since cave paintings, sex is a big part of *Second Life*. The virtual world is a haven where people

Mitch Wagner, "Sex in *Second Life*," *InformationWeek*, May 26, 2007. www.information week.com/news/showArticle.jhtml?articleID=199701944. Reproduced by permission of CMP Media LLC.

can fulfill their sexual fantasies by pretending to be the opposite sex, experimenting with homosexuality, owning a harem of sex slaves (who are themselves fulfilling their fantasies by role-playing as sex slaves), and more.

The sex is a sign that the virtual world is robust and thriving, said Philip Rosedale, founder and CEO of Linden Lab, the company that develops and operates *Second Life.*

"In a lot of ways, the presence of sex as an aspect of creative expression and playful behavior in a place like this is healthy, because it indicates we're doing something right," he said. The presence of sex is also a sign that people are engaging with the community and with each other, and connecting with each other as human beings, he added.

So how's it work, exactly?

Sex in *Second Life* starts with text chat. Participants describe what they're imagining doing with each other in graphic terms. Sometimes they talk to each other over Skype, or the phone. Soon, voice will be even easier in the virtual world—Linden Lab is beta-testing voice integrated into *Second Life,* and plans to roll it out over the next few months.

"100% of virtual sex is mental . . . so a professional here has to be a terrific manipulator of words and experience."

Of course, there's also a visual element. Users can buy outfits to dress their avatars provocatively, or "skins" to make them appear nude. Default avatars have no genitalia, so users need to buy them.

Likewise, users can buy equipment, ranging from realistic-looking beds and other furniture to fanciful torture devices used in BDSM fantasies. The furniture, and other props, have attached software—in *Second Life* jargon, they're "scripted"—to animate the user's avatar through the motions of sex. Sometimes, the script is attached to a simple sphere, called a "pose ball."

Leading vendors of *Second Life* genitalia and sex equipment include "Stroker Serpentine," the *Second Life* alter ego of Kevin Alderman, of Tampa, Fla., as well as Xcite!

Nudity and sexual behavior is forbidden in *Second Life* outside of private areas and sex clubs. Free orgy rooms are commonplace, where users can try out sexual apparatus and pose balls and bring their own.

Interview With A Virtual Madam

Escorts, the *Second Life* equivalent of phone-sex operators or prostitutes, are quite common in *Second Life*.

Tiffany Widdershins is owner of one of *Second Life*'s many bordellos. I met with her in her *Second Life* office, a replica of Bill Clinton's White House Oval Office. She offered me a cigar when I came in the room.

In addition to the Oval Office, her virtual bordello includes a bunny ranch modeled after a Vegas brothel, a locker room "complete with coach's office and showers," an area with a desert romance theme, and club and mall, she said.

"The stuff that really seems to go is the kinky stuff," says Widdershins. "This is the place that guys and ladies do the stuff that they secretly want to try in real life, but likely never will. I think it's because it has no real-life consequences," she said in text chat in-world.

Widdershins's avatar is a shapely woman, wearing a G-string, heels, and a sheer top. Her rear end is tattooed with the name of the business: LuvRags.

She started in the sex business in *Second Life* four months ago.

"One learns a lot about the truth of human nature from charging guys to pay for cartoon sex, and then watching them flock to it. 99% of people will tell you that they are against pornography, and yet it's 40% of online activity. The whole thing is pretty ridiculous, really," she said in a text-chat interview.

I asked her, "Why do you think people pay for it in *Second Life*? There doesn't seem to be a shortage of willing partners, and it's easy to look like a porn star."

The purpose of Second Life . . . *isn't amusement, it's commerce. "The fun is just the hook."*

She responded that the virtual escorts are better at it. "90% of sex is mental . . . and in fact 100% of virtual sex is mental . . . so a professional here has to be a terrific manipulator of words and experience," she said.

Many of her customers are looking for emotional intimacy they don't get in real life. "I have been paid to sit by a fire and listen to a guy pour his heart out," she said. . . .

Escorts charge 500 to 1,500 Linden dollars per session. That's about $2–$6. They pay Widdershins L$999 per month to wear the brand. She charges about L5,000 for her own services as a virtual escort, which she rarely does anymore.

In real life, Widdershins is semi-retired, having run a service that networks florists together. She asked that we withhold her real-life identity. She got into *Second Life* because she "smelled money."

"I looked to see where the best fit was for learning the economy here without any real skill sets," she said. "I am here to make a billion real life dollars, and I am just crazy enough to think it can be done."

The purpose of *Second Life*, she says, isn't amusement, it's commerce. "The fun is just the hook," she says. . . .

She's Been Doing Cybersex Nearly 20 Years

Jenna Leng has been looking for gratification online since just before she entered junior high school. She started on local BBSes in 1988.

"I was a good kid. Aside from the cybersex.;)" she said in an interview conducted through text chat in-world. But then she amended herself. "I wouldn't really call it cybersex. It was, strangely enough, cyber 'petting,' much of what normal teenagers do without the physical aspect. I talked about thoughts, or urges, kissing, touching. But again, that didn't head towards sex until much later."

She credits cybersex with helping her overcome early sexual repression. She says she is bisexual in real-life, and cybersex helped her overcome her sense of shame.

A multimedia designer from Los Angeles, she uses *Second Life* with the avatar name "Lienna Jael." When I teleported to interview her, she was wearing provocative bra and panties, but she quick-changed into a low-cut sundress for the interview.

Using her Lienna Jael pen name, she writes for Pixel Pulse, a *Second Life* adult blog that's also distributed in-world.

She enjoys exotic cybersex, "Hermaphrodites, shemales, alien avatars, futuristic cyborgs," she said.

She was accompanied by "Midori Akami," an avatar of a pretty brunette woman smoking a cigar—I was impressed by how realistic the smoke looked.

Akami said she doesn't use visualization or equipment much, preferring to rely on text. "Everybody's the same size in 12-point-type," she quipped. Her avatar, while adult, is half-sized. . . .

A Dark Side

But it isn't all fun and games.

German authorities are investigating simulated child molestation and real child pornography in *Second Life*. (Linden Lab says it will cooperate fully in the investigation.) They say a German TV station approached them with evidence that a 54-year-old man and 27-year-old woman were engaging in simulated sex in *Second Life*, one with an avatar that resembled an adult, another with an avatar that resembled a child. The

TV station also claimed to have downloaded a real child pornography image from *Second Life.*

Cybersex in *Second Life* involving adults playing the role of children has been a controversial part of the virtual world for a long time.

Cybersex in Second Life *involving adults playing the role of children has been a controversial part of the virtual world for a long time.*

Roleplay in general is integral to *Second Life*. Avatars appear to be beautiful men and women, elves, dragons, winged fairies, vampires, killer robots, and all varieties of other real and fanciful creatures.

Some residents choose to roleplay as children.

Some of that so-called "ageplay" is innocent, with the simulated children playing on jungle gyms, singing songs, and doing other things that real-life children do.

But some of the ageplay is sexual.

The ratio of innocent to sexual ageplay is about 50–50, said a leader in the ageplay community in an interview with the blog Second Life Herald in January.

The interview subject, who went by the name "Emily Semaphore" in *Second Life*, said she was a 35-year-old librarian in real life, and engages in both innocent and sexual ageplay with her real-life husband, who she met in *Second Life.* They managed an ageplay club called "Jailbait."

She said ageplay, both innocent and sexual, can help participants heal from the trauma of abusive childhoods. "I was molested for years by a family member. For me, roleplaying in a sexual manner is healing because it allows me to RECLAIM my sexuality," she said in the interview.

A *Second Life* resident and blogger who goes by the name "Tateru Nino" defends non-sexual ageplay and concludes by saying sexual ageplay between adults is nobody's business but the people involved.

But *Second Life* resident Catherine Fitzpatrick of New York, N.Y., said sexual ageplay, like other forms of sexual role-playing involving simulated coercion, is harmful.

"To pretend there is a firewall between *Second Life* and real life and that one has no effect on the other is infantile," said Fitzpatrick, a *Second Life* businesswoman who appears in *Second Life* as a male avatar named "Prokofy Neva."

Cybersex allows people to explore their sexual fantasies, some of which are physically impossible in real life, like men pretending to be women for sexual gratification.

Fitzpatrick's company, Ravenglass, leases server space from Linden Lab—known in *Second Life* jargon as "buying land"—and then rents it out. She says she does not allow erotic ageplay on her land.

Chris Peterson, a writer for the satirical Web site SomethingAwful.com, said he's visited ageplay areas in *Second Life* and was revolted by what he saw: "These were avatars of pre-pubescent children screaming in babytalk, 'Stop torturing me,' while individuals are doing unimaginable things. They're creating childish avatars that are four or five years old, and the sex acts are in a room covered with children's wallpaper," he said.

Fitzpatrick agreed. "We're not talking about 17-year-old girls with plaid skirts above their knees playing schoolgirl. We're talking about eight-year-olds being bound, whipped. It's extreme," she said.

Although Rosedale says sexual ageplay was always banned in *Second Life*, longtime residents say it was widespread until about January. Everybody knew about it. Then, in January, Linden Lab cracked down and started shutting down sexual ageplay areas.

Sex work in *Second Life* can often be exploitive, Fitzpatrick said. "These girls work, they work hard, and they don't get paid very much," she said. "There's a lot of people from developing countries. It attracts people who are unemployed." Sex work in *Second Life* also attracts stay-at-home Moms. "She can get in there, turn some tricks and hope that she's going to make enough to pay her gasoline money for a week," she said.

But other *Second Life* sex workers are just having fun, looking it as a way to pick up some extra money which they then spend in-world, she said. "I know people who are engineers, who get good salaries and have full lives, and they do prostitution in *Second Life* because they think it's fun and cool," she said. "Most of the ones I know who rent from me, or that I come across, they do prostitution to pay for the [in-world] shopping."

Sex advice columnist Dan Savage said . . . sex in *Second Life* is now being viewed with suspicion, as Internet dating and phone sex were initially. But *Second Life* sex, like Internet dating and phone sex, will become mainstream. It has its risks, but sex often does. "We've become acclimated to the risks and rewards of technologies as people apply them to sex, and all new technologies are applied to sex. Sex is always the leader," he said.

Cybersex allows people to explore their sexual fantasies, some of which are physically impossible in real life, like men pretending to be women for sexual gratification, Savage noted.

Second Life is also a place where people who are unattractive in real life can experience being attractive and sexually sought after, he said. . . .

Linden Lab Cracking Down

Until recently, Linden Lab didn't do much enforcement of rules on sexual activity in *Second Life*. But, spurred by European investigators, they've started cracking down on sexual ageplay.

And they recently announced plans to institute age verification, requiring content providers in *Second Life*—known in *Second Life* jargon as "land owners"—to flag adult content, and requiring residents to provide proof of age before being allowed to access adult content.

A *Second Life* resident who goes by the name "Gwyneth LLewelyn" said in a blog post that most participants in cybersex—especially patrons of *Second Life* sex businesses—will likely refuse to go through the validation process, and that will mean that sexual activity will be reduced drastically. Some professional content creators will be willing to take the privacy risks, and their remaining customers will be willing to pay more for high-quality content. The result: Sex in *Second Life* will become a lot less popular for amateurs and boutique businesses, and more of the domain of big businesses. . . .

People have sex in Second Life *because they have incredibly deep relationships, not just because they want to have sex.*

But Rosedale said the amount of sex in *Second Life* is often overestimated.

Linden Lab requires landowners to disclose if there's mature content on their land by checking a box on the control panel. As of Thursday, [May 24, 2007] about 15% of the land parcels in *Second Life* had that box checked, or 18% by land area, Rosedale said.

Moreover, not all that mature content is sexual in nature. When I first logged into the world, I thought it was. But I quickly learned that the "mature" rating is equivalent to the R rating for movies, not XXX. Simple use of swear words can get content flagged as mature.

"People's assessment of how much sex is going on in *Second Life* is overblown," Rosedale said.

Sex is simply not a huge part of *Second Life*, he said. If Linden Lab were to ban sex tomorrow—not that the company is thinking of doing that—the virtual world would continue on relatively unchanged. And, contrary to Fitzpatrick's speculation, Linden Lab would not suffer significant financial harm, he said. . . .

Linden Lab has taken harsh criticism from residents for the ageplay crackdown, and for cooperating in the investigation, but Rosedale stands by the decision.

He also questions the idea, put forward by Widdershins, . . . and others, that sex in *Second Life* is anonymous and without consequence.

Many people in *Second Life*—especially in the cybersex community—prefer to use the service without disclosing information about their real-life identities. In that respect, *Second Life* is anonymous.

But people do forge identities and relationships in *Second Life*. Friendship in *Second Life* involves real emotions, just as there can be a real emotional connection between pen pals who have never met.

Sex in *Second Life* often involves a relationship that evolves over time, Rosedale said.

"A lot of the sex relationships in *Second Life* are driven more by lengthy, meaningful discussions," Rosedale said. "People have sex in *Second Life* because they have incredibly deep relationships, not just because they want to have sex."

He added, "It isn't really an anonymous environment. It's really no more or less anonymous than the real world. If you want to travel to a faraway city where no one knows you and go into a strip club, that's anonymous too."

Second Life sex is a by-product of the sense of "presence" you get in-world, Rosedale said. That's something that's difficult to convey to anybody who hasn't used *Second Life* for more than a few hours. Presence pervades every element of *Second Life*, not just sex. When you're logged in to *Second Life* and your avatar is sitting across a table from another avatar, and you're discussing politics, it doesn't feel like you're alone at your computer—you have the illusion of really talking to another person across a table.

And sometimes when people are talking across a table, that leads to sex. In real life and in *Second Life*, too.

6

On-Screen Media Are Changing the Human Brain

Helen Phillips

Helen Phillips is a prize-winning science journalist specializing in neuroscience at New Scientist *magazine in England.*

The electronic age is changing the human brain. Some studies find that television and video games may increase intelligence by improving visual attention and problem-solving. Others suggest cyberspace amplifies natural personality traits, with the extroverts becoming more social and the introverted more isolated. The news about on-screen violence is generally bad, though, with high levels of television viewing increasing the likelihood that children will behave aggressively towards others. Furthermore, violent video games are more worrisome than TV because they are interactive, and children learn from being rewarded for getting things right.

Devin Moore was just 18 when he was taken to an Alabama police station for questioning about a stolen car. He was initially cooperative, but then lunged for his captor's gun. He shot the man twice and ran out into the hallway where he shot a second policeman three times. He let off five shots at a third man before making his escape in a police car. All three men died from shots to the head. When Moore was finally captured, he is reported to have said, "Life is like a video game. You have to die sometime." Two years on, he sits on death row.

Helen Phillips, "Mind-Altering Media," *New Scientist*, vol. 193, no. 2600, April 21, 2007. Reproduced by permission.

A civil case is being prepared by lawyers representing the victims' families, arguing that some responsibility for the crimes must be shared by Take-Two Interactive, publisher of the Grand Theft Auto game series; the Wal-Mart and GameStop stores for allegedly selling the games to an underage Moore; and Sony Computer Entertainment, maker of the PlayStation. Moore is said to have played Grand Theft Auto obsessively, and the families' lawyers will try to persuade the courts that the games trained him to murder. Effectively, they claim, he was faced with a real-life version of a scene he'd already played out many times.

While we have yet to see what the courts conclude, stories like this paint a gloomy picture of the media's influence on young minds. It may never be possible to prove that a specific act of violence was the result of a particular experience, but plenty of surveys and studies have linked poor media habits with rising violence, childhood depression, attention deficit disorders and declining educational standards. Yet we also hear entirely the opposite: IQ scores are rising, and have been since at least the 1950s, when television was becoming common in our homes. What's more, regular gamers seem to perform better at tests of visual attention and spatial awareness.

Any Technology Will Change the Brain

So what are the effects of modern media on the brain—especially young, developing brains? Are TV and computers boosting our mental and social networking skills, or making us stupid, isolated and aggressive, with the attention spans of gnats?

One thing researchers agree on is that any technology we use will change the brain. There's nothing surprising or sinister about this, says Martin Westwell at the University of Oxford's Institute for the Future of the Mind. "You are who you are largely because of the way the brain cells wire up in response to the environment and the things you do," he says.

"If you change the wiring you will change how we think." So how is the wiring changing?

It is impossible to conclude anything other than that violence on TV has raised the level of violence and aggression in our society—and while research on computer games has begun only recently, what there is suggests violent games have an even stronger effect.

Some say we're getting smarter. Steven Johnson, author of the book *Everything Bad Is Good for You*, argues that the increasing complexity of media presentations and games, with their multiple plots and sophisticated layers, requires more complex pre-planning and problem solving than ever. Far from dumbing us down, popular culture is stretching us, Johnson claims, and the rising IQ scores are a testament to that.

There is some evidence to support such claims. Shawn Green and Daphne Bavelier of the University of Rochester in New York have shown that regular computer gamers have improved visual attention and can take in more information. They are better able to pay attention to things that are further apart or more rapidly changing, and can switch attention more quickly. Even short-term play produces immediate improvements.

Jonathan Roberts of Virginia Polytechnic Institute found that women, who usually fare worse than men at spatial rotation tests, improve when exposed to 3D video games (whereas men did not) to the point where the sex difference disappears. Some physical abilities improve too. James Rosser of Beth Israel Medical Center in New York found that gaming experience is the best predictor of surgeons' skill at keyhole surgery—more so than the years spent training or the number of procedures carried out.

Rene Weber of the University of California, Santa Barbara, points out that TV too can be beneficial. "Many people know more about safe sex, AIDS and drugs from soaps than from the formal education system or books," he says, though the influence of this medium varies widely from person to person. More intelligent people learn just as well from books. Less intelligent people benefit from a more engaging presentation.

As for whether the Internet is making us more or less sociable, again it's a personal thing. Dmitri Williams of the University of Illinois at Urbana-Champaign has found that cyberspace amplifies our natural personality traits. The extroverts get even more social, and the introverted more isolated.

After watching just half an hour of violence, children have more devious and aggressive thoughts, are more likely to inflict punishments, and are less likely to cooperate.

Drawing general conclusions about the effect of the Internet is impossible, though, because it is so varied—from a source of information to a forum for chatting, playing games or being entertained. "Sometimes we are fairly passive viewers, other times we are up for a bit more of challenge. It is what we make it," Williams says.

More Bad News About Television

When it comes to TV, however, there's no getting away from the fact that the bad news outweighs the good. One of the biggest studies was done by Jeffrey Johnson and colleagues at Columbia University in New York, who followed more than 700 families for 17 years, recording their viewing habits, health, backgrounds and various behavioural tendencies. Their findings confirm those of previous, smaller studies showing that the amount of TV watched during childhood and teens correlates with changes in attention and sleep patterns, among other things.

The group's latest analysis will be published next month [May 2007] so Johnson can't reveal details yet, but says: "High levels of TV viewing may contribute to elevated risk for a type of syndrome which is often characterised by two or more of the following types of problems: elevated levels of verbal and physical aggression; difficulties with sleep; obesity and long-term risk for obesity-related health problems from a lack of physical exercise; and attention or learning difficulties."

One of the smaller studies, by Dimitri Christakls at the University of Washington in Seattle, found that young children watching double the average TV viewing hours (which were 2.2 per day at age 1 and 3.6 at age 3) were 25 per cent more likely to be diagnosed with attentional deficit hyperactivity disorder at age 7. Some research even hints at a link with autism, although this is very far from proven.

The overwhelming majority of studies about modern media and the mind, however, have focused on violence on and off the screen. Although there has been more than 50 years' worth of research, most people seem to have the idea that, while these studies suggest there might be a small link, the jury is still out. Wrong, says John Murray, a developmental psychologist from Kansas State University, one of the editors of the book *Children and Television: Fifty Years of Research* and author of U.S government–sponsored reports in 1972 and 1982. Murray is exasperated by this kind of ambivalence. He says it is impossible to conclude anything other than that violence on TV has raised the level of violence and aggression in our society—and while research on computer games has begun only recently, what there is suggests violent games have an even stronger effect.

"Video games are more worrisome than TV because they are interactive," says Murray. Children learn best by demonstration and then imitation, with rewards for getting things right. "That's exactly what video games do," he says.

Not everyone is affected, and we are not all affected in the same way, but overall, media violence does affect viewers' attitudes, values and behaviour, Murray says. Hundreds of studies demonstrate this, so why the doubt?

One reason is that media reports tend to give equal prominence to the naysayers. The debate also has its hired guns, with industry organisations such as the Motion Picture Association of America sponsoring prominent books arguing against any links. And whatever their motives, it is easy for critics to highlight the limitations of the science. The ideal experiment would be to divide a large number of children into groups, expose the different groups to different types or varying amounts of TV or computer games for several years while keeping all other experiences identical, and then to follow their progress for life. This will never be possible or ethical. Instead, researchers have to rely on long-term surveys that don't prove causality, and lab experiments that do not demonstrate long-term effects. Nevertheless, the results from all these different types of studies add up to a compelling case.

Modern media such as TV and computer games are changing our minds, and the more we are exposed to them the greater the changes. They are making us smarter and better at some tasks, but worse at others.

The Bobo Effect

One of the most straightforward demonstrations dates back to 1961, by Albert Bandura at Stanford University in Palo Alto, California. He showed short films to pre-schoolers. Half saw a man beating up a plastic clown. The other half saw more innocuous images. After watching the film, the children were allowed to play with all kinds of toys, including the doll. Those who had seen the beating went and punched it, even copying details like words the clown said. The Bobo doll studies show that children will imitate violent acts in precise detail.

It is not just children who are susceptible. This month a British man who had watched the horror film *Nightmare on Elm Street* 20 times was imprisoned after attacking another man with a home-made metal clawed glove, as happens in the film—one of many instances of copycat crimes.

Johnson's 17-year study shows a strong association between the amount of television watched during childhood and the likelihood of behaving aggressively towards others, even after compensating for other factors such as family background, previous aggression, neglect, neighbourhood and education. It's true that the causal relationship seems to run both ways—more aggressive people seem to watch more violent television—but this cannot explain the whole effect.

The findings show that television seems to raise aggression levels over time too. Young adults who had watched more than 3 hours of TV a day at age 14 committed five times as many aggressive acts—from threatening behaviour to actual physical assault—as those who watched less than 1 hour.

It's not just the obviously violent horror flicks and action movies that have this effect. Every hour of children's television portrays between 20 and 25 aggressive acts—more than on prime-time adult shows. Perhaps no wonder then that in the 1980s, Lesley Joy of the University of British Columbia in Canada and her colleagues showed that it doesn't matter whether the content is the best of public service broadcasting or the worst commercial drivel, it is the hours, not the content, that count.

Experiments in the lab have addressed the causal question, by dishing out particular viewing or gaming experiences followed by behavioural tests or questionnaires. This kind of study has shown that after watching just half an hour of violence, children have more devious and aggressive thoughts, are more likely to inflict punishments, and are less likely to cooperate.

Altered Responses

Brain imaging and other physiological measures also reveal changes in emotional responses to violent images as a result of viewing violence or playing violent games. Bruce Bartholow of the University of Missouri, Columbia, has found that people with a history of game playing have a reduced brain response to shocking pictures, suggesting that people begin to see such imagery as more normal. Another study found that frontal lobe activity was reduced in youngsters who played a violent video game for 30 minutes, compared with those playing an equally exciting but non-violent game. This brain region is important for concentration and impulse control, among other things. A region called the amygdala, important for emotional control, was more aroused in those who experienced the violent game.

Other studies show that children store memories of violent media acts in brain regions reserved for long-term storage of significant events. These memories can pop back into the mind very rapidly, even when not wanted, as flashbacks.

The effects fall into three categories, says Murray. There's a kind of imitation effect, where we seem to learn by example how to behave in certain situations. There's desensitisation, which means we become less shocked by and more tolerant of violence. Finally, there is the "mean world" effect, where people feel more vulnerable after seeing images of bad situations.

These effects are not always bad. Take desensitisation—if you're training medical students you want them to get used to gore, rather than vomiting when they see blood.

Our values, attitudes, family and education also work to mitigate the effects. Home life has a very big impact. If your family portrays attitudes that differ from the violence on TV, that really lowers the risk, says Joanne Cantor of the University of Wisconsin. "If you live in a violent area or abusive home, it increases the likelihood that violence will have an effect. But even kids with good things in life are affected. Maybe they will not be more violent but perhaps more hostile in their interpersonal relationships."

The big picture is clear. Modern media such as TV and computer games are changing our minds, and the more we are exposed to them the greater the changes. They are making us smarter and better at some tasks, but worse at others. And there is no getting away from the fact that on-screen violence fosters off-screen violence.

The tough question is what to do about it. No one is suggesting there are any simple solutions. Ultimately it all comes down to the choices we make as individuals or parents. If children are too busy playing sports or socialising to spend much time watching TV or playing games, and play something like Dr Kawashima's Brain Training when they do have time, the benefits will probably far outweigh any downside. For those who spend hour after hour playing shoot 'em ups or watching gorefests, the results for them—and others—could be dire.

7

Online Games
Can Be Addictive

Olga Khazan

Olga Khazan is a journalism student at American University in Washington, DC, and a special contributor to the Washington Post.

The game worlds of MMORPG's evolve constantly as players' actions influence the lives of other players' characters. This interaction with others can be so captivating that players never want to leave, to the detriment of their jobs, relationships, and health. Excessive online play has even led to death in a few cases. Game-addiction treatment programs are cropping up all over the world to help. Game-development companies deliberately set up games to be engrossing and lengthy but argue that time-consuming activities are not necessarily addictive.

They are war heroes, leading legions into battle through intricately designed realms. They can be sorcerers or space pilots, their identities woven into a world so captivating, it is too incredible to ever leave. Unfortunately, some of them don't.

Video games have often been portrayed as violence-ridden vehicles for teen angst. But after 10 people in South Korea—mostly teenagers and young adults—died last year [in 2005] from game-addiction causes, including one man who col-

Olga Khazan, "Lost in an Online Fantasy World: As Virtual Universes Grow, So Do Ranks of the Game-Obsessed," *washingtonpost.com*, August 18, 2006. www.washington post.com/wp-dyn/content/article/2006/08/17/AR2006081700625.html. Reproduced by permission of the author.

lapsed in an Internet cafe after playing an online game for 50 hours with few breaks, some began to see a new technological threat.

Participation in massively multiplayer online role-playing games, also called MMORPGs or MMOs, has skyrocketed from less than a million subscribers in the late 1990s to more than 13 million worldwide in 2006. With each new game boasting even more spectacular and immersive adventures, new ranks of gamers are drawn to their riveting story lines. Like gambling, pornography or any other psychological stimulant, these games have the potential to thrill, engross and completely overwhelm.

The Appeal of Interaction

The most widely played MMO, Blizzard Entertainment's World of Warcraft, has 6.5 million players worldwide, most of whom play 20 to 22 hours per week. Thousands can be logged in simultaneously to four different WoW servers (each its own self-contained "realm"), interacting with players across the globe in a vast virtual fantasy setting full of pitched battles and other violent adventures.

The main reason people are playing is . . . there are other people out there. . . . People know your name, they share your interests, they miss you when you leave.

Brady Mapes, a 24-year-old computer programmer from Gaithersburg, Md., and an avid WoW fan, calls it a "highly addictive game—it sucks the life out of you."

An MMO differs from an offline game in that the game world evolves constantly as each player's actions directly or indirectly influence the lives of other players' characters. In WoW, players can simply attack one another, interact with the environment, or role-play in more complex relationships.

More time playing means greater virtual wealth and status, as well as access to higher game levels and more-exciting content.

In addition, online gamers can join teams or groups (called "guilds" in WoW) that tackle game challenges cooperatively. Fellow team members see membership as a commitment and expect participation in virtual raids and other joint activities. The constant interaction with other players can lead to friendships and personal connections.

"The main reason people are playing is because there are other people out there," said Dmitri Williams, an assistant professor at the University of Illinois at Urbana-Champaign, who has researched the social impacts of MMOs. "People know your name, they share your interests, they miss you when you leave."

In MMOs, people lead wars and receive a lot of recognition. . . . It's hard to stop and go clean your room.

The Proliferation of Support Sites

As MMO fan sites filled with raving gamers proliferate, so have online-addiction help blogs, where desperate recluses and gamers' neglected spouses search for a way out.

"I don't want to do everything with [my husband], but it would be nice to have a meaningful conversation once in awhile," writes one pregnant wife on EverQuest Daily Grind, a blog for those affected by excessive use of another popular fantasy MMO. "He does not have much interest in the baby so far, and I am worried that after it is born, he will remain the same while I am struggling to work and take care of the baby."

Another gamer writes that she was angry at her boyfriend for introducing her to online gaming, which began consuming her life at the expense of her personal and academic well-being.

"But I think deleting [your] character doesn't work, because the game haunts you," she said. "All I could think about was playing."

Kimberly Young, who has treated porn and chat-room addicts since 1994 at her Center for Internet Addiction Recovery, said that in the past year [2006] video game fixation has grown more than anything else.

"In MMOs, people lead wars and receive a lot of recognition," Young said. "It's hard to stop and go clean your room. Real life is much less interesting."

The trend echoes across the continents, with game-addiction treatment centers cropping up in China in 2005 and this summer [2006] in Amsterdam. In South Korea, where 70 percent of the population has broadband Internet access, the Korea Agency for Digital Opportunity offers government-funded counseling for the game-hooked.

"Addicts want to live in a fantasy life because you can't do a 'do-over' in real life. . . . It can be hard to accept."

The games are set up to be lengthy, with a quest taking six hours or more to complete. The organization of players into cooperative teams creates a middle-school-esque atmosphere of constant peer pressure.

"You're letting other people down if you quit," Young said. "If you are good, the respect becomes directly reinforcing."

Why Gaming Can Become Excessive

According to research performed by Nick Yee, a Stanford [University] graduate student and creator of the Daedalus Project, an online survey of more than 40,000 MMO players, the average player is 26 years old; most hold full-time jobs. Seventy percent have played for 10 hours straight at some point, and about 45 percent would describe themselves as "addicted."

Yee believes escapism to be the best predictor of excessive gaming. A person who plays MMOs in order to avoid real-life problems, rather than simply for entertainment or socialization, is more likely to experience what he calls "problematic usage."

"People feel like they lack control in real life, and the game gives them a social status and value that they are less and less able to achieve in the real world," Yee said. "As a result, the real world gets worse and the virtual world gets better in comparison."

Liz Woolley, a Wisconsin software analyst and veteran of Alcoholics Anonymous, founded Online Gamers Anonymous in May 2002 by adapting AA's 12-step addiction recovery model to help gamers quit cold-turkey. Woolley recommends getting professional help for underlying issues and finding other hobbies and real-world activities to replace gaming.

"Addicts want to live in a fantasy life because you can't do a 'do-over' in real life," she said. "It can be hard to accept. You have to let them know, 'Hey, this is real life. Learn to deal with it.'"

"People are reluctant to point a finger at themselves," said Jason Della Rocca, executive director of the International Game Developers Association. Excessive use "is a reflection of friction in that person's life. They shouldn't use the game as a scapegoat."

Many in the industry are hesitant to call it an addiction because, in the case of MMOs, the nature of the problem is based on how it affects the user's life, not the amount of time spent playing.

Casual gamers may find it difficult to advance to the game's highest levels in the face of more dedicated rivals, such as Mapes, the Gaithersburg WoW fan, whose highest-level warrior character is a force to be reckoned with. "If I go up against someone who only plays for one to two hours, I'll decimate them," he said. "There are other games out there if you only want to play a couple hours at a time."

That dedication sometimes pushes Mapes to see the game as more of a chore than a pastime. "Sometimes I realize that I'm not having any fun, but I just can't stop," he said.

The Strategies of Game Development Companies

Several of the MMO researchers interviewed for this story pointed out that many game companies employ psychologists who analyze the games and suggest ways to make them easier to play over long stretches of time.

Della Rocca argues that because online games' monthly subscription rates remain constant regardless of how many hours a subscriber spends on the network, developers profit less when gamers play more intensively.

The psychologists "monitor subjects playing the games in order to eliminate flaws and points of frustration," Della Rocca said. "The notion that we are trying to seduce gamers is a fabrication of people who don't understand how games are developed."

Since Blizzard Entertainment released WoW in 2004, calls to Online Gamers Anonymous have more than tripled, according to Woolley, who said the industry is directly at fault for the suffering of the people she tries to help.

"I think the game companies are nothing more than drug pushers," she said. "If I was a parent, I wouldn't let them in my house. It's like dropping your kids off at a bar and leaving them there."

The signs of excessive MMO use are similar to those of alcoholism or any other dependency—tolerance, withdrawal, lying or covering up, to name a few. However, many in the industry are hesitant to call it an addiction because, in the case of MMOs, the nature of the problem is based on how it affects the user's life, not the amount of time spent playing.

According to tvturnoff.org, Americans spend an average of 28 hours a week watching television, a fact that has yet to spawn a bevy of dependence clinics.

"If a person was reading novels excessively, we'd be less likely to call that 'addiction' because we value reading as culture," said the University of Illinois's Williams. "We see game play as frivolous due to our Protestant work ethic. There's plenty of anecdotal evidence out there to suggest this is a problem, but it's not the role of science to guess or bet."

The Choice to Stop Playing

Mapes, who has played other engrossing titles such as Medal of Honor and Diablo and eventually set them aside, said the decision to control excessive gaming is one any player can make.

"Ultimately, every player has a choice to stop," he said. "I've stopped before, and I've seen other people stop if they get burned out."

Woolley disagrees, especially after witnessing the bitter outcome of her son's EverQuest obsession.

Shawn had played online games before, so she didn't suspect anything different when he picked up the newest MMO from Sony. Within months, Woolley said, Shawn withdrew from society, losing his job and apartment and moving back home to live a virtual life he found more fulfilling.

After a number of game-induced grand mal seizures sent Shawn, who was epileptic, to the emergency room repeatedly, he chose to pay ambulance bills rather than stop playing. The medical professionals he saw treated his external symptoms but dismissed his gaming condition.

"They told me, 'Be glad he's not addicted to something worse, like drugs,' and sent him home," Woolley said.

On Thanksgiving Day 2001, Woolley found 21-year-old Shawn dead in front of his computer after having committed suicide. EverQuest was on the screen.

Readers' responses to an article written about the incident in a local Wisconsin paper poured in, and the national attention Shawn's story subsequently received prompted Woolley to start up a self-help Web site. In the four years since its launch, Online Gamers Anonymous (www.olganon.org) has had 125 million hits and registered more than 2,000 members, Woolley said.

"I realized that gaming addiction was an underground epidemic affecting thousands of people, but no one was talking about it," she said. "I wasn't worried about pressure from the gaming industry. I thought, 'You already took my kid, you can't take anything else.'"

8

Seriously Ill Children Get Information and Support from Online Games

Marissa Levy

Marissa Levy writes about health and education for the national daily newspaper USA Today.

Serious illnesses such as cancer, cystic fibrosis and sickle cell anemia can be frightening and confusing for children, but an international non-profit organization dedicated to lifting the spirits of seriously ill children is using a game format that children enjoy to help them learn about their diseases. The Starlight Starbright Children's Foundation released several interactive video games online to help touch more seriously ill children and to make it easy to keep the information in the games up to date. Health professionals caution, though, that such games are removed from real-life experience and should not be used as a substitute for face-to-face psychological support.

Serious illness such as cancer, cystic fibrosis and sickle cell anemia can be frightening and confusing for children, but the Starlight Starbright Children's Foundation wants to help educate today's tech-savvy kids about these diseases in a way that appeals to them: through the Internet.

With almost a third of online gamers under age 18, it's no surprise that most children turn to their computer screens for entertainment. So Starlight tapped into this growing interest,

Marissa Levy, "Online Games Lift Spirits of Seriously Ill Kids," *USA Today*, November 6, 2006, p. 7D. www.usatoday.com/tech/gaming/2006-11-06-starlight-games_x.htm. Copyright 2006, USA Today. Reprinted with permission.

and this summer it made eight of its games available free online to help children who suffer from serious diseases educate themselves in a fun and interesting way.

Online Games with a Special Purpose

The digital games, which were developed in 2001 but were not available on CD-ROM until now [November 2006], provide school-age kids with "basic disease concepts, pain management and coping techniques and skills for communicating pain to adults," according to the foundation, a non-profit organization that provides support to seriously ill children and their families.

The Starlight offerings are just the latest in a string of interactive games that are designed to help children come to grips with disorders that grip their bodies.

"Kids love the interactivity, getting information in a format they like using as opposed to reading a pamphlet."

According to *Children's Technology Review*, almost 100 games aimed at educating kids about their health and wellness have moved onto the interactive virtual gaming scene since 1994, and many of them can be accessed free online.

- *Ben's Game*, which is offered in nine languages from the Make-A-Wish Foundation's San Francisco Bay Area chapter, allows kids to destroy mutated cancer cells to help visualize beating their diseases. The game offers three levels of difficulty, and players can customize their own protagonist.

- The Charles and Helen Schwab Foundation website features six games and other interactive tools such as blogs and sound mixers to help children with dyslexia connect with other learning-disabled children and learn to manage their disorders.

69

- *Mystery of the Rash Outbreak*, based on the 2001 animated movie *Osmosis Jones*, takes players inside the human body in the role of a white blood cell detective on a mission to stop an infectious rash.

Joan Ford, Starlight's vice president of strategic initiatives, says online trivia games such as Starlight's *The Sickle Cell Slime-O-Rama Game* and *Uncovering the Mysteries of Bone Marrow* make it easy for children to understand their diseases.

Slime-O-Rama, for example, uses colorful graphics and questions to test players on their knowledge of sickle cell disease, a chronic blood disorder that alters the shape of red blood cells, causing pain and tissue damage. The interactive game doles out advice such as how to deal with pain episodes, how many glasses of water to drink a day and why the disease is not contagious.

Warren Buckleitner, editor of *Children's Technology Review*, which provides product reviews for child-oriented interactive media, calls the Starlight games "a terrific poster child for how to use the Web to help children understand specific (health) conditions."

Says Ford, "Kids love the interactivity, getting information in a format they like using as opposed to reading a pamphlet."

The online format also allows the foundation to update the content of the games with the latest medical information. And with the wide reach of the Internet, the Starlight Foundation can touch more children who have serious diseases. Ford says more than 25 other websites provide links to the Starlight games.

"It's good for kids to have direct knowledge about what affects them," says Osbia Jones, program coordinator for the South Central Pennsylvania Sickle Cell Council, which distributes Starlight's *Slime-O-Rama* to its members. "It's a way to be self-actuating and begin the process of taking control of their health early."

Games as Learning Tools

Buckleitner says interactive video games are effective learning tools because they allow children to feel empowered.

But the games, which Buckleitner calls "images on glass," are removed from real-life experience, which goes against one of the fundamental aspects of learning, especially for children, he says. Health professionals caution that online games should be just one of many tools parents use to help their children deal with a serious illness.

Donald Schifrin, communications chairman of the American Academy of Pediatrics, says that although the field of educational Internet games is "blossoming," parents shouldn't turn to interactive games as a substitute for face-to-face psychological support.

"(Online games) are part of the healing process for youngsters but shouldn't be the only pursuit. There is more progress when the entire family is involved in the therapeutic process," Schifrin says.

Tonya Hodge, 42, whose son Jaylen, 12, has sickle cell disease, says she started playing *Slime-O-Rama* about a year ago on CD-ROM, but now that the game is online, she likes to play it more often to refresh her memory about Jaylen's condition.

"(The game) helps me understand," Hodge says. "I like to see if I know what I'm talking about."

Jaylen says he plays *Slime-O-Rama* every once in a while and believes the online games have helped him understand his disease better. He even seems to have it out for *Slime-O-Rama*'s host. What's his favorite part? "When you get to slime him!"

9

Children's Isolation from the Natural World Is a Threat to Their Health

Richard Louv

Richard Louv is the author of seven books about family, nature, and community. In addition to his column for the San Diego Union-Tribune, *he has written for the* New York Times *and other newspapers.*

Today's children are increasingly disconnected from the natural world, for multiple reasons, including society's growing affection for electronic media. Mental, physical, and spiritual health, though—especially that of children—depend on being able to use all the senses, to experience the wonder of nature.

Not that long ago, the sound track of a young person's days and nights was composed largely of the notes of nature. Most people were raised on the land, worked the land, and were often buried on the same land. The relationship was direct.

Today, the life of the senses is, literally, electrified. One obvious contributor is electronics: television and computers. But simpler, early technologies played important roles. Air-conditioning, for example: The U.S. Census Bureau reports that in 1910, only 12 percent of housing had air conditioning. People threw open their sash windows and let in night air and the sound of wind in leaves. By the time the baby boomers

Richard Louv, *Last Child in the Woods: Saving Our Children from Nature-Deficit Disorder*, Chapel Hill, NC: Algonquin Books, 2005. Reproduced by permission.

came along, approximately half our homes were air-conditioned. By 1970, that figure was 72 percent, and by 2001, 78 percent.

In 1920, most farms were miles from a city of any size. Even by 1935, fewer than 12 percent of America's farms had electricity (compared to 85 percent of urban homes); not until the mid-1940s were even half of all U.S. farm homes electrified. In the 1920s, farmers gathered at feed stores or cotton gins to listen to the radio, or created their own wired networks by connecting several homes to a single radio. In 1949, only 36 percent of farms had telephone service.

Losing Our Senses

Few of us are about to trade our air conditioners for fans. But one price of progress is seldom mentioned: a diminished life of the senses. . . . As human beings we need direct, natural experiences; we require fully activated senses in order to feel fully alive. Twenty-first century Western culture accepts the view that because of omnipresent technology we are awash in data. But in this information age, vital information is missing. Nature is about smelling, hearing, tasting, seeing below the "transparent mucous-paper in which the world like a bon-bon is wrapped so carefully that we can never get at it," as [English writer] D. H. Lawrence put it, in a relatively obscure but extraordinary description of his own awakening to nature's sensory gift. Lawrence described his awakening in Taos, New Mexico, as an antidote to the "know-it-all state of mind," that poor substitute for wisdom and wonder:

> Superficially, the world has become small and known. Poor little globe of earth, the tourists trot round you as easily as they trot round the Bois or round Central Park. There is no mystery left, we've been there, we've seen it, we know all about it. We've done the globe and the globe is done.
>
> This is quite true, superficially. On the superficies, horizontally, we've been everywhere and done everything, we know

all about it. Yet the more we know, superficially, the less we penetrate, vertically. It's all very well skimming across the surface of the ocean and saying you know all about the sea. . . .

As a matter of fact, our great-grandfathers, who never went anywhere, in actuality had more experience of the world than we have, who have seen everything. When they listened to a lecture with lantern-slides, they really held their breath before the unknown, as they sat in the village school-room. We, bowling along in a rickshaw in Ceylon, say to ourselves: "It's very much what you'd expect." We really know it all.

We are mistaken. The know-it-all state of mind is just the result of being outside the mucous-paper wrapping of civilization. Underneath is everything we don't know and are afraid of knowing.

Urban children, and many suburban children, have long been isolated from the natural world because of a lack of neighborhood parks, or lack of opportunity. . . . But the new technology accelerates the phenomenon.

Some of us adults recognize the know-it-all state of mind in ourselves, sometimes at unlikely moments.

Todd Merriman, a newspaper editor and father, remembers an illuminating hike with his young son. "We were walking across a field in the mountains," he says. "I looked down and saw mountain lion tracks. They were fresh. We immediately headed back to the car, and then I saw another set of tracks. I knew they had not been there before. The lion had circled us." In that moment of dread and excitement, he became intensely aware of his surroundings. Later, he realized that he could not remember the last time he had used all of his senses so acutely. The near encounter jarred something loose.

How much of the richness of life have he and his son traded for their daily immersion in indirect, technological experience? Today, Merriman often thinks about that question—usually while he is sitting in front of a computer screen. . . .

The Rise of Cultural Autism

In the most nature-deprived corners of our world we can see the rise of what might be called cultural autism. The symptoms? Tunneled senses, and feelings of isolation and containment. Experience, including physical risk, is narrowing to about the size of a cathode ray tube [computer monitor], or flat panel if you prefer. Atrophy of the senses was occurring long before we came to be bombarded with the latest generation of computers, high-definition TV, and wireless phones. Urban children, and many suburban children, have long been isolated from the natural world because of a lack of neighborhood parks, or lack of opportunity—lack of time and money for parents who might otherwise take them out of the city. But the new technology accelerates the phenomenon. "What I see in America today is an almost religious zeal for the technological approach to every facet of life," says Daniel Yankelovich, the veteran public opinion analyst. This faith, he says, transcends mere love for new machines. "It's a value system, a way of thinking, and it can become delusional."

The late Edward Reed, an associate professor of psychology at Franklin and Marshall College, was one of the most articulate critics of the myth of the information age. In *The Necessity of Experience* he wrote, "There is something wrong with a society that spends so much money, as well as countless hours of human effort—to make the least dregs of processed information available to everyone everywhere and yet does little or nothing to help us explore the world for ourselves." None of our major institutions or our popular culture pay much notice to what Reed called "primary experience"—that which we can see, feel, taste, hear, or smell for ourselves. According to Reed, we are beginning "to lose the ability to experience our world directly. What we have come to mean by the term experience is impoverished; what we have of experience in daily life is impoverished as well." [seventeenth-century philosopher] René Descartes argued that physical reality is so ephemeral that humans can only experience their personal, internal interpretation of sensory input. Descartes' view "has become a major cultural force in our world," wrote Reed, one of a number of psychologists and philosophers who pointed to the post-modern acceleration of indirect experience. They proposed an alternative view—ecological psychology (or ecopsychology)—steeped in the ideas of John Dewey, America's most influential educator. Dewey warned a century ago that worship of secondary experience in childhood came with the risk of depersonalizing human life.

Much of our learning comes from doing, from making, from feeling with our hands, and though many would like to believe otherwise, the world is not entirely available from a keyboard.

North Carolina State professor Robin Moore, director of the National Learning Initiative, takes Reed and Dewey to heart in his contemporary examination of postmodern childhood play. Primary experience of nature is being replaced, he writes, "by the secondary, vicarious, often distorted, dual sensory (vision and sound only), one-way experience of television and other electronic media." According to Moore,

> Children live through their senses. Sensory experiences link the child's exterior world with their interior, hidden, affective world. Since the natural environment is the principal source of sensory stimulation, freedom to explore and play with the outdoor environment through the senses in their own space and time is essential for healthy development of an interior life. . . . This type of self-activated, autonomous

interaction is what we call free play. Individual children test themselves by interacting with their environment, activating their potential and reconstructing human culture. The content of the environment is a critical factor in this process. A rich, open environment will continuously present alternative choices for creative engagement. A rigid, bland environment will limit healthy growth and development of the individual or the group.

Emotional Implications of New Technologies

Little is known about the impact of new technologies on children's emotional health, but we do know something about the implications for adults. In 1998, a controversial Carnegie Mellon University study found that people who spend even a few hours on the Internet each week suffer higher levels of depression and loneliness than people who use the Net infrequently. Enterprising psychologists and psychiatrists now treat Internet Addiction, or IA as they call it.

Even as we grow more separate from nature, we continue to separate from one another physically. The effects are more than skin deep, says Nancy Dess, senior scientist with the American Psychological Association. "None of the new communication technologies involve human touch; they all tend to place us one step removed from direct experience. Add this to control-oriented changes in the workplace and schools, where people are often forbidden, or at least discouraged, from any kind of physical contact, and we've got a problem," she says. Without touch, infant primates [the group of animals that includes monkeys, apes and humans] die; adult primates with touch deficits become more aggressive. Primate studies also show that physical touch is essential to the peacemaking process. "Perversely, many of us can go through an average day and not have more than a handshake," she adds. Diminishing touch is only one by-product of the culture of technical control, but Dess believes it contributes to violence in an ever more tightly wired society.

Frank Wilson, professor of neurology at the Stanford University School of Medicine, is an expert on the co-evolution of the hominid hand and brain; in *The Hand*, he contends that one could not have evolved to its current sophistication without the other. He says, "We've been sold a bill of goods—especially parents—about how valuable computer-based experience is. We are creatures identified by what we do with our hands." Much of our learning comes from doing, from making, from feeling with our hands; and though many would like to believe otherwise, the world is not entirely available from a keyboard. As Wilson sees it, we're cutting off our hands to spite our brains. Instructors in medical schools find it increasingly difficult to teach how the heart works as a pump, he says, "because these students have so little real-world experience; they've never siphoned anything, never fixed a car, never worked on a fuel pump, may not even have hooked up a garden hose. For a whole generation of kids, direct experiences in the backyard, in the tool shed, in the fields and woods, has been replaced by indirect learning, through machines. These young people are smart, they grew up with computers, they were supposed to be superior—but now we know that something's missing."

The Infinite Reservoir

Not surprisingly, as the young grow up in a world of narrow yet overwhelming sensory input, many of them develop a wired, know-it-all state of mind. That which cannot be Googled does not count. Yet a fuller, grander, more mysterious world, one worthy of a child's awe, is available to children and the rest of us. Bill McKibben, in *The Age of Missing Information*, argues that "the definition of television's global village is just the contrary—it's a place where there's as little variety as possible, where as much information as possible is wiped away to make 'communications' easier." He describes his personal experience with a nearby mountain: "The mountain says you live in a particular place. Though it's a small area, just a square mile or two, it took me many trips to even start to learn its secrets. Here there are blueberries, and here there are bigger blueberries ... You pass a hundred different plants along the trail—I know maybe twenty of them. One could spend a lifetime learning a small range of mountains, and once upon a time people did."

Any natural place contains an infinite reservoir of information, and therefore the potential for inexhaustible new discoveries. As Robert Michael Pyle says, "Place is what takes me out of myself, out of the limited scope of human activity, but this is not misanthropic. A sense of place is a way of embracing humanity among all of its neighbors. It is an entry into the larger world."

During my visits with middle school, high school, and college students, a discussion of the senses would inevitably come about when we talked about nature. Sometimes I would ask directly, other times the students would raise the subject in the classroom or later, through essays. Their verbal answers were often hesitant, searching. This was apparently not a subject that many, if any, had confronted before. For some young people, nature is so abstract—the ozone layer, a faraway rain forest—that it exists beyond the senses. For others, nature is simple background, a disposable consumer item. One young man in a Potomac, Maryland, classroom described his relationship with nature as shaky, at best. "Like most I exploit what it gives and I do with it what I please," he said. He thought of nature "as a means to an end or a tool. Something made to be used and admired not something to live. Nature to me is like my house or even like my cluttered room. It has things in it which can be played with. I say play away, do what you want with it, it's your house." He made no mention of the senses, saw or understood no complexity. I admired his honesty.

Yet other young people, when prompted, did describe how experiences in nature excited their senses. For example, one boy recalled his sensory experience when camping, "the red and orange flames dancing in the darkness, the smoky fumes rising up, burning my eyes and nostrils. . . ."

Surely such moments are more than pleasant memories. The young don't demand dramatic adventures or vacations in Africa. They need only a taste, a sight, a sound, a touch . . . to reconnect with that receding world of the senses.

The know-it-all state of mind is, in fact, quite vulnerable. In a flash, it burns, and something essential emerges from its ashes.

10

Electronic Interaction Is Making Americans Less Literate

Jeremy Rifkin

Jeremy Rifkin is the author of The Age of Access *and many other books about the impact of scientific, technological, and cultural changes on the economy, society, and the environment.*

People all over the world are preoccupied with developing new technologies for communicating with one another, but while people are communicating more, they seem to be having more trouble expressing themselves. Furthermore, future generations seem doomed to lose emotional attachments with their fellow human beings. To help with this problem, researchers are trying to develop computerized virtual characters who can recognize human emotions and respond accordingly. Such technological pretensions are both sad and frightening.

Over the past 20 years or so [since 1986], we have been preoccupied with developing new ways of communicating with each other. Our cellphones, computers, Blackberries, text messaging, e-mail and the Internet connect 25 percent of the human race in a speed-of-light global village.

At the same time that we are connecting the central nervous system of our species in an electronic embrace, the human vocabulary is plummeting all over the world, making it more difficult to express ourselves. It appears that we are all communicating more, but saying less.

Jeremy Rifkin, "Virtual Companionship," *International Herald Tribune*, October 11, 2006. Reproduced by permission of the author.

Declining Literacy, Growing Loneliness

According to a national survey conducted by the U.S. Department of Education [DOE], English literacy among college graduates has declined dramatically in the past 10 years [since 1996]. Only 31 percent of college graduates today are proficient in English literacy, compared with 40 percent just a decade ago. Grover J. Whitehurst, the director of the DOE Institute responsible for overseeing the National Assessment of Adult Literacy, said that he believes that literacy is declining as a result of the increase in television viewing and surfing the Internet.

Worse, it seems the more connected we are in our electronic landscapes, the lonelier we find ourselves. A study by the Kaiser Family Fund showed that American children now spend an average of 6.5 hours per day watching television, surfing the Internet, text messaging and playing with video games and other electronic media. More worrisome, the study found that most children interact with electronic media alone.

Our children are losing the emotional attachments that come with face-to-face participation with their fellow human beings. Nor are American youngsters an anomaly. Children in other high-tech countries are following close on the heels of their American peers. This new condition can be described as the "high-tech blues."

Virtual High-Tech Blues

Are future generations to be forever lonely? No, say the technological optimists. Engineers at some of the leading technology centers are feverishly working on the next generation of technological marvels to address our lonesome high-tech existence. The field is called "affective computing" and the goal is to create technology that can express emotion, interpret and respond to the emotions of their human handlers, and even establish a sense of intimacy with their human companions. Built-in cameras allow the computers to detect even subtle changes in facial expressions, which are then processed in real time, allowing the computer to recognize the emotional state of the person.

A growing number of young people find themselves enmeshed in virtual worlds where make-believe substitutes for real-life experience.

Rosalind Picard, one of the pioneer researchers in the field of "affective computing," reports on a study done at the [Massachusetts Institute of Technology] MIT Media Lab. A computerized virtual person named "Laura" plays the role of an exercise adviser, helping real-life subjects. Laura is capable of conversing and is able to use hand gestures, eye-gaze behavior, posture shifts, head-nods and facial expressions. Laura, like any good exercise trainer, provides feedback on their performance, helps them improve on their regimen, and gives empathetic verbal and facial feedback.

The reactions of the subjects are revealing. Compared with subjects interacting with a "non-relational" computer interface, a number of the subjects—but not all—working with Laura reported an emotional rapport similar with what one might expect with a real-life trainer.

Other experiments conducted at Stanford University report similarly positive results with empathetic embodied computer agents interacting with subjects, leading researchers to conclude that "embodied computer agents are indeed social actors in the truest sense of the word 'social,' capable of forming relationships with users comparable to those found in the world of human-human interactions."

It's hard to know whether to laugh off such technological pretensions as sadly pathological or whether to be truly frightened. There is no doubt that a growing number of young people find themselves enmeshed in virtual worlds where make believe substitutes for real-life experience. With "affective computing" looming on the horizon, the truly lonely can look forward to interacting with silicon companions, programmed to empathize and even care.

Progress? Surely we can do better.

11

Experts Disagree Whether Online Games Have Educational Value

Sarah Glazer

Sarah Glazer is a specialist in health, education, and social-policy issues whose articles have appeared in the Washington Post, Glamour, Public Interest, *and* Gender and Work, *a book of essays.*

Some scholars claim online games are good for literacy, problem-solving, learning to test hypotheses, and researching information from a variety of sources. Others say gaming may be good for understanding technical information but not for reading literature and understanding the humanities. Enthusiasts claim gaming is preparing young people for the knowledge-based workplace. Critics worry that it is making kids more socially isolated, less experienced in working with others, and less creative.

On a hot summer afternoon, eight teenagers gathered in the darkened basement of the Bronx Central Library to play the top-selling football video game "Madden NFL." The Madden tournament in the Bronx, complete with prizes, is part of a growing effort at libraries across the country to lure a client who rarely darkens the door of a public library—the adolescent boy.

"If it wasn't for the gaming stuff dragging me in that first time, I would have gone maybe once in the past two years,"

Sarah Glazer, "Video Games," *CQ Researcher*, vol. 16, no. 40, November 10, 2006, pp. 937–960. Copyright © 2006 by CQ Press, published by CQ Press, a division of Congressional Quarterly Inc. All rights reserved. Reproduced by permission.

says Ian Melcher, 17, a gamer in Ann Arbor, Mich., who had just checked out two calculus books. "I realized the library was pretty cool and had other things I was interested in."

To persuade skeptical libraries to put video games on the shelf next to books, young librarians who grew up on games are drawing support from a surprising source—academic researchers. They claim that playing video games is practically a requirement of literacy in our digital age.

A New Form of Literacy

To many parents and baby boomers, playing video games looks like mindless activity. Yet the knowledge built into "Madden," for example, employs a playbook the size of an encyclopedia. To win, players must have a sophisticated understanding of strategy, and make split-second decisions about which play to choose.

When you strip away all the explosions, blood, magic coins, princesses and castles, video games are problem-solving tasks.

"Games stress taking your knowledge and applying it. That's pretty crucial in the modern world," says University of Wisconsin professor of reading, James Gee, author of the 2003 book *What Video Games Have to Teach Us about Learning and Literacy.*

Indeed, the argument that video and computer games are superior to school in helping children learn is gaining currency in academic circles. Claimed benefits include improved problem-solving, mastery of scientific investigation and the ability to apply information learned to real-life situations. Some of the more complex games, especially multiplayer games like "World of Warcraft"—played online simultaneously with thousands of players—lead some teens to engage in esoteric, online conversations about strategy and to create their own literary spinoffs or so-called fanfiction.

"Many video games require players to master skills in demand by today's employers," concluded a report released in October by the Federation of American Scientists, citing complex decision-making and team building. The organization urged the federal government to invest in research and development of educational games for K-12 students and for adult workforce training.

Science writer Steven Johnson, who popularized the pro-game argument in his 2005 book *Everything Bad Is Good for You*, argues that when a child enters the world of a computer game, he is "learning the scientific method" as he tries out multiple hypotheses. For instance, today's youngsters don't first sit down and read a rule book, the way baby boomers did. They start pushing buttons to see what happens.

Despite the worries of baby-boomer parents, there's no evidence that video gaming is replacing reading among teens.

A Unique Boost for Entrepreneurship

That willingness to learn from failure uniquely prepared members of the dot-com generation, giving them an advantage as entrepreneurs and creative thinkers in the new economy, argue business experts John C. Beck and Mitchell Wade in their 2004 book *Got Game*. "A kid in the classroom has to worry about looking like an idiot. In a game, they're raising their hand all the time, and true learning comes from failing," concurs Dmitri Williams, assistant professor of speech communication at the University of Illinois at Urbana-Champaign. "When you strip away all the explosions, blood, magic coins, princesses and castles, video games are problem-solving tasks—puzzles. There's some irony in the fact that kids are bored at school but rush home to solve these games where they learn math and history."

As evidence that kids are willing to master language and concepts usually considered over their head, Johnson describes an hour spent teaching his nephew to play the urban planning-style game "SimCity." While Johnson was trying to figure out how to save a dying industrial neighborhood, the 7-year-old piped up, "I think we need to lower industrial tax rates."

"SimCity" creator Will Wright says the youngster probably didn't understand tax rates any more than baby boomers understood mortgages when they played "Monopoly" as kids. But he thinks games teach something else. "The ability to reverse-engineer in your head a model of some arbitrarily complex thing is an incredibly valuable skill that you can apply to almost anything in this world," he says, whether that's doing your taxes, programming a new cell phone or predicting the effect of global warming.

"To claim that learning magic spells is good preparation for the knowledge-based workplace is just plain silly."

Despite the worries of babyboomer parents, there's no evidence that video gaming is replacing reading among teens. According to a Kaiser Family Foundation survey, reading for pleasure has remained steady in the past five years even as video-gaming time has risen.

But what about teens who seem to spend most of their leisure time on games? Heavy gamers—more than an hour a day—actually spend more time reading for pleasure (55 minutes daily) than teens who play no video games at all (41 minutes), according to the Kaiser survey. And Kaiser found only 13 percent of adolescents were heavy gamers. . . .

Questionable Educational Value

Not all scholars are equally enthusiastic about the learning value of video games on the market. In most games, the content is "garbage," according to Harvard Graduate School of Education Professor Christopher Dede, "in the sense that it deals with imaginary situations that are not close to the knowledge and skills people need for the 21st century. To claim that learning magic spells is good preparation for the knowledge-based workplace is just plain silly."

Dede is among those interested in adapting one of the most popular offshoots of gaming—virtual worlds—to educational aims. Players create characters (or avatars) who enter a virtual world. Hundreds of thousands of teenagers now participate in virtual worlds like There.com and Second Life, where they can create a character, buy clothes and real estate and meet other players' avatars.

In "River City," created by Dede's team at Harvard, players try to figure out the cause of a mysterious epidemic in a 19th-century town. Researchers found that middle-schoolers using "River City" improved their biological knowledge and science skills more than peers taught more traditionally.

Another sign of university interest: Colleges now offer courses in "Second Life." Starting this fall [2006], teens entering There.com will be able to take classes in areas like copyright law taught by university professors.

Students remember only 10 percent of what they read and 20 percent of what they hear but almost 90 percent if they do the job themselves, even if only as a simulation.

But some advocates worry that all this high-level learning will be limited to middle-class kids, who have access to fancier, faster hardware and to educated parents who can guide their choice of games—creating a new equity gap on top of the existing reading gap between income groups. . . .

Fostering Creative Thinking

For the past year, nearly two-dozen 8-to-13-year-olds from low-income neighborhoods in Madison, Wis., have gathered after school to play the bestselling game "Civilization," under the watchful eyes of University of Wisconsin researchers. Players rule a society from 4000 B.C. to the present, building cities, trading, gathering natural resources, and waging war. A single game requires about 20 hours to play; achieving high-level mastery requires 100 hours or more.

The children encounter words like "monarchy" and "monotheism" for the first time—but more important, they have to figure out how those and other factors, like natural resources, help a civilization survive or fail, says Kurt Squire, an assistant professor of educational communications and technology, who is directing the study.

"We found when they're expert gamers, they can tell you the differences between civilizations, what technologies they would need, what resources they'd need," he says. To Squire, the game's lifelike simulation is a powerful twist on the progressive-education adage, learning by doing.

Students remember only 10 percent of what they read and 20 percent of what they hear but almost 90 percent if they do the job themselves, even if only as a simulation, according to research cited by the Federation of American Scientists. The University of Wisconsin's Gee even claims that the mind works like a video game in that "effective thinking is more like running a simulation" than forming abstract generalizations.

"It bothers me that people are using these [video games] as the great way of learning. They're a modest alternative to very bad teaching."

An academic camp led by Gee argues video games foster a more sophisticated kind of literacy than the simple decoding of words. Video games foster creative thinking—producing "gaming literacies" in the words of Katie Salen, a designer at Parsons, The New School for Design in New York City. Gamers not only follow the rules "but push against them, testing the limits of the system in often unique and powerful ways," she says.

Digital literacy also means learning to take information from multiple sources, including Web sites and other players, rather than from one authoritative source like a teacher or textbook. . . .

Mastering Technical Language

Parents often despair because their teen is "not sitting on a couch reading a storybook, which is what we think literacy is," says Gee. But "the kids' version of literacy is better for a modern-world understanding of technical language," Gee maintains.

In the best games, players must master a specialized game vocabulary, consulting Web pages for hints on winning that probably use syntax far more complex than their reading in school, Gee argues. "I believe firmly the key to school success is handling technical language," he says.

To see how complex the language can get, Gee suggests looking at a Web site offering hints on playing "Yu-Gi-Oh" (both a video and card game). A typically impenetrable sentence reads, "The effect of 8-Claws Scorpion is a Trigger Effect that is applied if the condition is correct on activation." Seven-year-olds are reading sentences like this, even though its complexity won't be matched in the classroom until middle or high school, Gee says.

But can games produce the kind of literacy we most value? The technical material highlighted by enthusiasts is closer to technical manuals than novels and "more likely to appeal to techies than to dreamers, humanists, and conversationalists" and to boys rather than girls, worries Harvard Professor of Cognition and Learning Howard Gardner. Immersing oneself in long novels like *Madame Bovary,* in poetry or in a philosophical text involves a skill many game enthusiasts disparage—linear thinking over many pages. That's "an entirely different mental faculty than is exploited when one surfs the Web from one link to another," Gardner argues.

"You play 'World of Warcraft'? You're hired!" Someday these words may be spoken by employers—if they're not already.

Moving Away from Passive Learning

Moreover, even a good video game can't compete with a great teacher, asserts former teacher Joan Almon, coordinator of the Alliance for Childhood in College Park, Md. "It bothers me that people are using these as the great way of learning. They're a modest alternative to very bad teaching," she says.

In its recent report, however, the Federation of American Scientists urges teachers to change from their "tell and test" method—which encourages passive learning—to incorporating the highly interactive, challenge-reward environment of video games. Game developers have incorporated the best learning features recognized by cognitive science, the report says, including:

- tons of practice;

- continual monitoring and feedback on the player's progress;

- encouragement to seek out information on the game strategy from other gamers, friends, and Web sites; and,

- bridging the gap from what's learned to real situations.

Some enthusiasts point out that the Internet is already allowing teenagers to become online creators on a huge scale via blogs, music, and mini-films known as *machinima*—often inspired by games. Players have posted several hundred-thousand stories ranging from 10-page plots to small novels as part of the bestselling computer game of all time, "The Sims," where players create their own family and play virtual house. . . .

A Total-Immersion Course

"You play 'World of Warcraft'? You're hired!" Someday those words may be spoken by employers—if they're not already—two technology experts wrote in *Wired*, praising multiplayer games for teaching important workplace skills.

In "Warcraft," players band together in guilds to share knowledge and manpower in a "quest," such as slaying monsters. To run a large guild, a master must be able to recruit new members, create apprenticeship programs, orchestrate group strategy and settle disputes. One young engineer at Yahoo used to worry about whether he could do his job. "Now I think of it like a quest," he said. "By being willing to improvise, I can usually find the people and resources I need to accomplish the task."

Indeed, becoming a guild master "amounts to a total-immersion course in leadership," argue John Seely Brown, former director of Xerox's Palo Alto Research Center, and Douglas Thomas, an associate professor of communication at the University of Southern California's Annenberg School for Communications.

Business experts Beck and Wade came to similar conclusions after surveying 2,100 young professionals, mainly in business. In their book *Got Game*, they claim those with extensive gaming experience were better team members, put a high value on competence, and had more potential to be superior executives. Perhaps most important, they argue, gamers understand that repeated failure is the road to success. They found that 81 percent of those under age 34 had been frequent or moderate gamers.

In their most provocative assertion, Beck and Wade claim the dot-com phenomenon was "structured exactly like a video game" in that it called for entrepreneurial skills and a fearlessness toward failure in a generation that grew up gaming. Among the rules learned from gaming were:

- If you get there first, you win;

- Trial and error is the best and fastest way to learn;

- After failure, hit the reset button; don't shrink away.

As Stanford researcher Yee has discovered, many players view playing multiplayer online games as work. Players in "Star War Galaxies" who pick pharmaceutical manufacturing as a career must decide how to price and brand their products, how much to spend on advertising, and whether to start a price war with competitors or form a cartel with them. Once players acquire the skills to be competitive in the market, their business operations require a daily time commitment.

Video games could increase the speed at which expertise is acquired, improve players' ability to apply learning and improve decision-making—all important for the coming "conceptual economy."

Better than Traditional Schooling

Yet today's schools, obsessed with reading and writing, are preparing children for jobs that soon will be outsourced overseas, claims David Williamson Shaffer, associate professor of learning science at the University of Wisconsin-Madison. "The only good jobs left will be for people who can do innovative and creative work," he writes, arguing that video games that teach professional-level language can accomplish that task better than traditional schooling.

A Federation of American Scientists report recently [as of 2006] endorsed that view, urging government, industry, and educators to take advantage of video-game features to "help students and workers attain globally competitive skills." It said video games could increase the speed at which expertise is acquired, improve players' ability to apply learning and improve decision-making—all important for the coming "conceptual economy."

Already gamers are running political campaigns, negotiating treaties, and building environmentally sensitive communities, the report notes. Ashley Richardson was a middle-schooler when she ran for president of Alphaville, the largest city in the popular multiplayer game, "The Sims Online." She debated her opponent on National Public Radio in her campaign to control a government with more than 100 volunteer workers, which made policies affecting thousands of people.

By contrast, students who pass typical school tests often can't apply their knowledge to real-life problems, according to research cited by Shaffer. Students who can write Newton's laws of motion down on a piece of paper still can't use them to answer a simple problem like "If you flip a coin into the air, how many forces are acting on it at the top of its trajectory?" . . .

No Substitute for Social Learning

Some critics worry that the game-playing 20-something generation never gained some of the socialization skills and creativity needed in the workplace. The Alliance for Childhood's Almon doubts that chatting online in a multiplayer game can substitute for face-to-face interaction.

"We've been told by one software company that they have to spend so much time teaching the young 20s how to work with others because they've grown up in isolation," she says. The way children traditionally developed those problem-solving skills was by creating their own play situations with one another, which were "extremely complex, nuanced and filled with social learning, problem-solving, and creativity," she says. But children don't do that much independent play anymore, she observes.

Some enthusiasts counter that video games can turn gamers into little scientists who have to figure out the rules on their own. Simulation games like "The Sims" help in mastering sciences that utilize computer-based simulation, including biology and cognitive science, suggests the University of Wisconsin's Gee.

But Harvard's Dede is skeptical. "Do kids learn some things about taking a confusing situation and puzzling about it? Sure, but we wouldn't need schooling if learning was as simple as just putting people into experience and letting them figure it out," he says. "That's just as true for gaming experiences as for real-world experiences." The key is to adapt the methods developed for entertainment to educational games so they can be "a powerful vehicle for education."

12

Online Games Will Have an Impact on the Economy

Edward Castronova

Edward Castronova is associate professor of telecommunications at Indiana University and an expert on the economies of virtual worlds.

The sales of online video games will continue to rise for some time, as more computer-savvy young people mature and increase the demand. The supply of online games will also grow, but at an uneven rate, because of the high initial costs and long development time involved in world-building. The long-run outlook is that online games may provide significant competition to other areas of the economy. This phenomenon is already apparent in declining television viewing among certain population segments.

Most analysts predict that sales of video games will rise rapidly for some time, led by the online component of gaming. We're also seeing an increase in the usage of nongame synthetic worlds and avatar-mediated communication systems in general. Analysts argue that the increases can be extrapolated for a number of years; as high-speed Internet and wireless technologies enmesh the globe, the assumed latent demand for these products and technologies will express itself in rising sales. . . .

It seems quite likely that each of the next two or three generations will each be more involved in synthetic worlds than its immediate predecessor.

Edward Castronova, *Synthetic Worlds: The Business and Culture of Online Games*, Chicago, IL: University of Chicago Press, 2005. © 2005 by The University of Chicago. All rights reserved. Reproduced by permission.

How Demand Will Grow

How will this growth actually manifest itself? First, it is important to emphasize the generational component in the adoption of these technologies. Because synthetic worlds are among the most intensive applications of new media technology, there is a steep learning curve in using them. People seem to have no problem, however, if they have grown up with computers, pagers, cell phones, and video games. Those of a certain age, on the other hand, find the whole thing baffling. As time passes, a larger fraction of the population will fall into the former category and the demand for synthetic world access will gradually grow.

The significant word in that prediction is *gradual*: unless something dramatic changes in the user interface of these worlds, their growth will not be like the twentieth century's rapid adoption of revolutionary media such as television. The penetration rates will differ because of the difference in learning curves. You operate a television by turning two knobs. One knob gets a moving picture going. The other changes what picture you get to see. If you're hard of hearing, there's a third knob that makes it louder. [Anyone] could operate a TV. And that meant that TV was able to expand throughout the world's population as fast as RCA and Zenith could make CRTs. Not so with synthetic worlds. Driving an avatar in hostile conditions is a skill that takes time to learn. While there is some chance that the spread of gaming console systems with online functionality—which make an effort to reduce the plethora of buttons and levers one must master to get by in these places—will speed up the growth rate, it will probably not have a significant effect. Much of what is new in a synthetic world does not involve the interface. Negotiating the embedded social system takes time; this is a party in a play, not a moving picture. As a result, one should not expect explosive growth in this sector.

Moreover, on the supply side, the growth will almost certainly not be steady. Rather, it will follow the boom-bust-boom pattern of many new technologies. As I write this [2005], there are one or two dozen obviously successful synthetic worlds in operation, but perhaps over 100 in development. The year 2003 saw a number of highly touted new worlds fall flat; if this is a growth sector, one might ask, why are so many of the latest additions doing poorly?

When Ultima Online *and* EverQuest *had their success in the late 1990s, everyone and his avatar decided to make a world.*

Worlds Cost a Great Deal to Make

On the one hand, this is perhaps a moment to remember Carl Jung's dictum: "One of the most difficult tasks men can perform, however much others may despise it, is the invention of good games." Making a game that is this big, this complex, and also fun, for thousands and thousands of people playing with *each other*, is surely a great creative and intellectual challenge. A more specific explanation, however, has to do with the nature of synthetic world development and its cost and revenue structure. Note, for example, that we have only seen a very few of these places close their virtual doors. That is an extraordinary fact in an industry where 95 percent of the titles are expected to fail and disappear within weeks. The trend in MMORPGs is completely different: the world is developed for three to five years, released, and then maintained seemingly forever. A flop in this market is not a world that closes down—with rare exceptions, none of them do that—it is a world that lives on but does not have many subscribers.

This pattern can be traced to the unique nature of costs and revenues from world-building: Worlds cost a great deal to make but not as much to run. Meanwhile, most revenue comes from subscription fees after the world is built. As a result, it does not take much in the way of subscription revenue to overcome ongoing operation cost. Once a world is open, then, you might as well keep it open, because ongoing operations bring net revenue to the company. For a world to be *profitable*, however, that stream of net operating revenue has to eventually overcome the large capital cost of building the world in the first place. When a world falls flat on arrival, the net revenue from subscriptions is a trickle, not a stream, and the whole project, while still alive, has turned out to have been a losing proposition. This has been the fate of several new worlds as of this writing [2005], and will undoubtedly be the fate of many more. Indeed, by the time this book is published, it would not surprise me to find that the market for synthetic worlds is being described as a complete bust, yet another new-media hoax, hokum, and hype.

> *Even in a down market . . . there is room for success.* Blizzard's World of Warcraft *broke single-day PC game sales records at its release.*

The Boom-to-Bust-to-Boom Cycle

I would argue against that view; rather, these developments are a natural pattern for any good with this combination of cost, revenue, and demand. Demand grows slowly in this space, probably more slowly than technological innovation on the supply side. When these worlds first appeared, the first few were obviously very profitable. When *Ultima Online* [UO] and *EverQuest* had their success in the late 1990s, everyone and his avatar decided to make a world. Building a world takes several years, and when all the post-*UO* worlds spilled onto the market four years later, there was a glut: the demand for worlds had risen by perhaps 50 percent while the number of worlds went up 500 percent. But because you don't need many subscribers to keep a world going, none of the weaker worlds have closed their doors. Thus the market recently has seen dozens of cancellations and poorly received new releases, punctuated every six months by a genuine success. Meanwhile, the global numbers continue to increase, quarter by quarter. Each new success seems to add its population to the industry without detracting significantly from the population of current entrants; otherwise, older worlds like *UO* would have folded long ago. This indicates that the demand must be increasing, but growing less rapidly than supply.

Even in a down market, on the other hand, there is room for success. Blizzard's *World of Warcraft* broke single-day PC game sales records at its release on November 23, 2004. As this book goes to press, it is on target to reach several hundred thousand subscribers.

TV viewing among 18–34-year-old males has fallen by more than 10 percent in the viewing seasons 2002–2003 and 2003–2004.

Whatever trauma this boom-to-bust-to-boom cycle may induce in the development community and the popular press, in fact, all is well from the consumer's standpoint. The economist and sage Joseph Schumpeter (1945–1984) long ago alerted us to the fact that the best thing about an evolving economic system is that it destroys mediocre things. Therefore, let there be a glut of worlds, and may the best worlds win. The quality and quantity of available fantasy worlds are both clearly rising. The fact that the market falls into a boom-and-bust cycle, especially at the start, should not blind anyone to the long-run forces behind this technology.

Competitors That May Be in Trouble

Focusing on the long run, then, where do synthetic worlds fit into the economy? Here are some competitors that may be in trouble:

Passive Media Entertainment

Many gamers say that playing games only required cutting one thing out of their lives: TV. Data from Nielsen Media Research indicate that TV viewing among 18–34-year-old males has fallen by more than 10 percent in the viewing seasons 2002–2003 and 2003–2004; Burbank [California city, home to many media companies] wonders where they have gone, but Austin [Texas] (the center of the multiplayer gaming industry) knows. And if we were to return to the 1970s and tell contemporary pundits that the new century would see many people abandoning their TV sets in favor of an interactive and social form of entertainment, I'm sure they would have jumped for joy. The glory days of that horrid car-selling box in your living room are perhaps over. Indeed, DVR recording technology is turning it into an interactive medium itself. Other forms of passive media—films, books, spectator sports—might be affected too. The open question here is whether the average person would really rather be doing something than watching it.

Travel and Tourism

When Tahiti is only a few clicks away, why take a flight there? When I already own a ship that can fly me to Alpha Centauri, why support a space program that's just getting to Mars? This is not to say that NASA's work is unimportant work; I'm only pointing out that its support in the populace may weaken as fantasy space travel starts to feel more and more like the real thing, without the costs and complications.

Communications

Avatar-to-avatar communication can offer everything that voice communication can, and it also offers facial expression and body language. It requires less bandwidth to communicate gestures than video does. Moreover, people may prefer to have a simulated self do the talking rather than the real thing. And avatars are a very intuitive way to implement social software: with an avatar interface, not only can we both write on the white board that appears on your computer and mine, we can also gesture to it. And with an avatar, you can mingle in a space. No other technology offers the same superior combination: all of the good things about face-to-face communication, with none of the bad.

User Interfaces

Running a computer is still rather difficult today. The wizard who answers to your click on "set up new network connections" is a wizard in name only. Why not make him a real wizard, with a gray beard and a pointy starred hat, who sets up connections for you when you ask him to? That would certainly be more intuitive than clicking and typing and clicking and typing. As for daily work tasks, a person connected to an avatar can have the avatar summon a virtual typewriter and open a virtual mailbox. If there's a problem, the user can get some help by talking to an AI in avatar form. There are already synthetic worlds with embedded email, instant messaging, and web access. There seems to be little that we do with our computers that we could not do in avatar form. And we may prefer the avatar form for numerous reasons; perhaps it is the most intuitive way to translate body gestures into commands.

In sum, depending on the preferences of average people, synthetic worlds may make an impact in several important areas of the economy.

13

Crime in Virtual Worlds Is Impacting Real Life

Tim Guest

Writer Tim Guest lives in London, England, and has contributed to the Guardian *and* Daily Telegraph *newspapers.*

When around 30 million people log in to virtual worlds each week, it is no surprise that some break the law. Virtual items are beginning to acquire real-world value, driven in part by players who want to advance quickly in online games without having to spend hours in the process. As virtual crime starts to spill over into the real world, however, games companies and legal and law enforcement authorities are being forced to decide where legitimate game play ends and real law-breaking begins and to impose appropriate penalties.

As murders go, it was an open and shut case. In February last year [2005], Qiu Chengwei, a 41-year-old man from Shanghai, loaned his prized sword, called a dragon sabre, to his 26-year-old friend Zhu Caoyuan. Without telling Qiu, Zhu sold it for 7200 yuan [$950], pocketing the proceeds. Qiu complained to the police that Zhu had stolen his sword, but they refused to help. So early one morning a month later, Qiu broke into Zhu's house and stabbed him to death.

Qiu confessed to police, and a few months later was sentenced to life imprisonment. But while the murder was quickly solved, the question of whether Zhu was guilty of theft is still

Tim Guest, "Just a game?" *New Scientist*, vol. 190, no. 2552, May 20, 2006, pp. 38—42. Copyright © 2006 Reed Elsevier Business Publishing, Ltd. Reproduced by permission.

[as of 2006] unsettled. In the trial, the court heard that the police refused to help Qiu because in their eyes Zhu hadn't broken any laws—the sword wasn't real. It was a virtual weapon that Qiu's character gave Zhu's in an online fantasy game called Legends of Mir, which has over a million players.

The murder is one of a string of similar cases in which virtual crimes have spilled into the real world. It is a phenomenon that has caught players, games companies and police forces off guard, and they are just beginning to experiment with ways to deal with it. The consensus is to settle disputes and punish bad behaviour inside the game if at all possible. To do this some players have organised virtual mafias to help other players get even, and recently some games companies have begun meting out justice themselves by banishing the evil-doing characters to what is effectively a virtual jail, and even crucifying them.

Lawbreaking Is No Surprise

When you consider the number of people playing these games, it is perhaps not surprising that some break the law. Each week, around 30 million people worldwide abandon reality for imaginary realms with names like EverQuest, EVE Online and World of Warcraft. While there have always been games that encourage "criminal" behaviour as part of the game, there has been a big change recently. What you do in the game can now make real money, and lots of it.

"It's like the Wild West right now, and we're kind of like these outlaws. I feel like Billy the Kid."

Virtual items began to acquire a real-world value when new players wanted to advance quickly in these games without having to spend hours looking for weapons or gaining magical powers. This created a grey market for rare virtual goods, first on eBay and then on scores of other websites set up to help this trade. Soon, exchange rates between game money and real currencies emerged that have helped line the pockets of thousands of players.

For example, in 2004, in a game called Project Entropia, David Storey of Sydney, Australia, bought a virtual island populated by virtual wild animals for $26,500—not for fun, but for profit. He now charges a tax for virtual hunting rights, and rents virtual beachside property, from which he has already earned $10,000. Earlier this month [May 2006], Mind-Ark, Project Entropia's developer, blurred the boundary between the virtual and the real worlds still further when it launched a cash card players can use at ATMs around the world to withdraw money against their virtual hoards, calculated according to the Project Entropia exchange rate. In 2004 IGE, a virtual item trading website based in Boca Raton, Florida, estimated the global market in virtual goods to be worth around $880 million a year and growing. When this kind of money is involved, it's a fair bet that from time to time virtual crime is going to turn into the real thing.

And games are full of virtual crimes. Mafia men, pimps, extortionists, counterfeiters and assassins populate various virtual worlds, eager to make a fast buck. There's even a terrorist collective in one game hell-bent on bringing about the end of their own online world. Most keep their activities confined to the virtual, but the line is becoming increasingly blurred.

No Laws Against Virtual Crime

Take the tale of Istvaan Shogaatsu—an infamous character in EVE Online, a space piracy game—played by dental technician Tom Czerniawski from Toronto, Canada. Shogaatsu is the CEO of Guiding Hand, a mercenary corporation that destroys other players' characters for profit. Czerniawski describes him as "a cut-throat without morals or mercy."

In May 2005, Czerniawski/Shogaatsu was contacted with an anonymous offer of 1 billion ISK—the Eve currency, worth around ... [$700] when traded in the real world—for a "Pearl Harbor" style attack on another player's corporation, Ubiqua Seraph. Arenis Xemdal, Guiding Hand's "valentine operative" played by Bojan Momic, also of Toronto, spent four months wooing the head of Ubiqua, known as Mirial, who then hired him. To make Xemdal look good, Shogaatsu staged raids deliberately intended to fail, and four months later Mirial appointed Xemdal as her trusted lieutenant. She handed him the access codes to Ubiqua's warehouses: the key to her virtual safe.

It was time for Shogaatsu and his associates to make their move. A Guiding Hand battleship appeared near Mirial's position. She fled for a nearby space station, but before she could reach safety, Xemdal turned his lasers on her. Across the galaxy, Guiding Hand operatives looted six warehouses. Shogaatsu delivered Mirial's corpse to the client, but kept the stolen property as spoils of war.

The EVE developers, CCP, based in Reykjavik, Iceland, looked fondly on Istvaan's operation—not least because, as the story spread through the Internet, the game gained thousands of new subscribers. But many players were outraged. After the heist, Czerniawski received nine email and telephone death threats. The cash and merchandise stolen by Guiding Hand amounted to 30 billion ISK—about ... [$20,000]. To Mirial and others connected with the Ubiqua Corporation, the loss felt very real.

The incident shone a bright light on the frontier-style ethos of many games. It had taken Mirial over a year to build up her virtual empire, but she had no recourse: no laws protect her players from virtual losses. Games developers need it to remain that way, as they want to keep their responsibility to a minimum. Gaming would be unsustainable if every unpleasant act became punishable in the real world.

In spite of this, Czerniawski told me he and his Guiding Hand co-conspirators were concerned they might be accused of committing a real-world crime, such as wire fraud, so to avoid this they were careful to keep all contact within the game.

Taking Crime Beyond Virtual Boundaries

What happens when the distinction between actions inside the game and outside it is less clear? For example, is exploiting a bug in a game to make hard cash breaking the rules? In December 2004, Noah Burn, a 24-year-old from Myrtle Beach, South Carolina, did just that in EverQuest II.

In the real world Burn worked as a furniture salesman. So when he got bored of his exploration of the virtual world, he set up a "furniture" store inside the game. His character, a barbarian called Methical, found places to buy desirable virtual goods cheaply and then sold them at a profit. One afternoon he put a chair up for auction—this normally removes the item from the virtual world. Later that day he got a message from someone who had bought the chair, but when he looked over to his virtual showroom, the chair was still there. Sitting at his computer, Burn realised he had stumbled on a gold mine. He quickly sent a message to his friends online: "I think I just duped [duplicated] something". Burn had discovered a bug in the game's code which meant he could "dupe" items at will. Selling real furniture pays well, he says, "but not as well as in EverQuest II".

> *Linden Lab called in the FBI, in what is probably the first criminal investigation of activities that originated inside a virtual world.*

Along with a friend, Burn set up a production line, copying expensive candelabras that players used to decorate their virtual homes. After a day of trading, they had two virtual platinum pieces—at a time when one platinum piece sold for $300. The next night they duped, Burn says, "until our eyes bled". Bored with candelabras, they switched to a virtual animal called a Halasian Mauler dog, the highest value item they could dupe. In virtual terms, the two were rich. They bought virtual mansions, the best spells and the most expensive horses they could find.

Then they took a step out of the game and began to sell the proceeds of their virtual counterfeiting for dollars. Burn knew he was doing something questionable and every day expected Sony, the owner of EverQuest II, to fix the bug. Two weeks later they were still selling, now at 50 per cent of the market rate, just to shift more platinum. They were scammed too: they lost $5,000 when buyers took their items without paying. But they kept on selling. They sold so much virtual currency that prices dropped 60 per cent. Burn made so much money that he decided to consult a lawyer to see if he was breaking the law. The lawyer threw up his hands. "He had no idea what I was talking about."

Companies are starting to accept that some sort of policing is necessary. As a rule, the medieval approach prevails—those who break the rules are suspended, or exiled from the virtual world.

Players began to post complaints about the sudden inflation on various web forums. Then three weeks after he discovered the bug, Burn logged on to find it had been fixed. Their spree was at an end. Burn says his little cabal made $100,000 in total, of which he got the lion's share. "It has allowed me to go to Hawaii and Paris, as well as pay off student loans," he says.

Sony banned some of Burn's accounts the next day, but there was no way of working out which items were counterfeit and so no way of penalising him. "It's like the Wild West right now, and we're kind of like these outlaws," Burn says. "I feel like Billy the Kid."

Real Consequences—and Real Protection

Burn may have made real money, but the consequences of his actions were confined to the game world. Others have bridged the gap between the two. Between October and December last year [2005] a group of residents in a game called Second Life—who cannot be named for legal reasons—experimented with attacks on the fabric of the Second Life universe itself. They constructed self-replicating objects which copied themselves over and over until the whole universe became overcrowded and the game's servers crashed. One group even created an object resembling a block of virtual Semtex [a plastic explosive]. Just like a real bomb, when it exploded, the servers running that section of the universe went down, destroying the realm and everything in it.

Linden Lab, which runs Second Life, says the attacks cost the company time and money and were a clear violation of US Code Title 18, section 1030—which outlaws "denial-of-service" attacks. The law says, in effect, that if you knowingly transmit information to a computer involved in communication beyond the boundaries of the state that results in $5,000 or more of damage, you face a hefty fine and up to 10 years' imprisonment. Linden Lab called in the FBI, in what is probably the first criminal investigation of activities that originated inside a virtual world. "These attacks affect the ability of our servers to provide a service for which people are paying us money," says Ginsu Yoon, Linden Lab's counsel.

In Linden Lab's eyes, at least, planting a virtual bomb should be considered a real crime.

In April, he spent seven days nailed to a cross for ruthlessly killing new players as soon as they entered the game.

It's not only the games companies that say in-game crimes have real consequences. The player who owned Mirial spent a large amount of time and effort amassing her virtual wealth. Its theft and her character's murder was a tangible loss. Cases like these only serve to emphasise that the issue of ingame justice is becoming a serious concern.

To date, the absence of law enforcement inside these games has led to players setting up their own alternatives. Jeremy Chase, a customer service manager and IT specialist based in Sacramento, California, formed the Sim Mafia within the game Sims Online. Players could hire Chase and his virtual employees to perform all the services you might expect from a bona fide crime family.

As the popularity of Sims Online waned, Chase moved his crime family to another game run by Linden Lab, a free-form universe called Second Life, where he renamed himself Marsellus Wallace. Now, for the right amount of virtual currency, Chase's family will "sort out" any problems you have with another Second Life resident. . . . In the real world Chase's mafia activities would pit him against the law. Online, Wallace is well known to Linden Lab and has become a minor celebrity within the game. For now he continues to act with impunity.

Laying Down the Virtual Law

But slowly, things are changing. For many people, online gaming is now a major part of life—a third of Second Life players spend more time in the game than in the real world. So companies are starting to accept that some sort of policing is necessary. As a rule, the medieval approach prevails—those who break the rules are suspended, or exiled from the virtual world. Linden Lab now runs a points system: the more frequently you misbehave and the worse the transgression, the more negative points you get. The higher the rate at which you accrue points, the more severe the punishment. "Violations that target other characters or make Second Life feel unsafe or unwelcoming are dealt with more aggressively," says Linden Lab's Daniel Huebner.

Banishment is a blunt tool, however, as players can simply creep back into the game under another name and identity. And in any case, the issue of punishment per se throws up a tough question for games companies: isn't the point of the virtual worlds to escape the restrictions of the real one?

So Linden Lab is testing an alternative approach of rehabilitating offenders. In January, Second Life resident Nimrod Yaffle reverse engineered some computer code to help him steal another player's virtual property. He was reported and became the first resident to be sent to a new area of the game, The Cornfield—a kind of virtual prison. Every time he logged on all he could do was ride a virtual tractor and watch an educational film about a boy who drifts into a life of crime.

Other games are also trying to keep punishments in tune with their setting. For example, Cynewulf, played by an electrical engineer from Flint, Michigan, is perhaps the only American alive who has some experience of crucifixion. He is a resident of a new game called Roma Victor, which is based in Roman Britain, and a barbarian. In April [2006] he spent seven days nailed to a cross for ruthlessly killing new players as soon as they entered the game.

The punishment had an effect. "It was surprisingly agonising for just being a game," Cynewulf says. "Being jeered at by the Romans while immobilised is not much fun. Particularly since they are all weaklings who deserve to die by my sword."

Acts like Cynewulf's virtual murders can usually be clearly labelled as crimes. But what about more subtle forms of disagreement? What if your neighbour builds a huge tower block that blocks the light to your virtual garden? Who can you turn to? Last year, two law students, known in Second Life as Judge Mason and Judge Churchill, decided to solve this problem by opening the Second Life Superior Court. Residents could take their arguments, large or small, to the in-world courtroom. With reference to the Second Life rules, and their own knowledge of real-world law, the judges would resolve disputes.

Predictably, not all Second Life residents liked the idea. "What a mind-numbingly futile exercise," Tony Walsh wrote on a Second Life bulletin board. "So now we have yet another level of tedious bureaucracy to Second Life." Others wondered whether the court would have any teeth to back up a judgement, or even what would happen if a Linden (a character played by an employee of Linden Lab) was the target of a case. To clarify their non-involvement, Linden Lab requested that the court change its name. It is now the Metaverse Superior Court. With its teeth removed, the court fell into disuse. The idea isn't totally dead: there is one small community in Second Life, called New Altonburg, that successfully polices itself. Linden Lab would like more communities to handle their own disputes, and its wish may not be that far-fetched.

If crime in the online community continues to flourish, expect the laws and regulations of the real world to eventually catch up with residents of Second Life and other virtual worlds. When that happens, you can bet it won't be long before they start wishing for a third life to escape to.

14

Online Gamers Have no Recourse for Lost Wealth or Rights

Cory Doctorow

Cory Doctorow is a columnist for InformationWeek, *as well as a blogger, Internet activist, and science fiction writer.*

Online games are like absolute dictatorships, where the whim of the companies controlling them is law. If players have conflicts with game management, any wealth they have built up in the game can vanish. However, if someone were to create a "democratic" virtual world that provided the protections of true citizenship and the prerequisites for building stable wealth, it is likely that only one component would be missing: fun.

Can you be a citizen of a virtual world? That's the question that I keep asking myself, whenever anyone tells me about the wonder of multiplayer online games, especially Second Life, the virtual world that is more creative playground than game.

These worlds invite us to take up residence in them, to invest time (and sometimes money) in them. Second Life encourages you to make stuff using their scripting engine and sell it in the game. You Own Your Own Mods—it's the rallying cry of the new generation of virtual worlds, an updated version of the old BBS adage from the WELL: You Own Your Own Words.

Cory Doctorow, "Why Online Games Are Dictatorships," *InformationWeek*, April 16, 2007. http://www.informationweek.com/story/showArticle.jhtml?articleID=199100026. Reproduced by permission of CMP Media LLC.

I spend a lot of time in Disney parks. I even own a share of Disney stock. But I don't flatter myself that I'm a citizen of Disney World. I know that when I go to Orlando, the Mouse is going to fingerprint me and search my bags, because the Fourth Amendment isn't a "Disney value."

Disney even has its own virtual currency, symbolic tokens called Disney Dollars that you can spend or exchange at any Disney park. I'm reasonably confident that if Disney refused to turn my Mickeybucks back into U.S. Treasury Department-issue greenbacks that I could make life unpleasant for them in a court of law.

In-world wealth is like a Stalin-era dacha, or the diamond fortunes of Apartheid South Africa: valuable, even portable (to a limited extent), but not really yours, not in any stable, long-term sense.

But is the same true of a game? The money in your real-world bank account and in your in-game bank account is really just a pointer in a database. But if the bank moves the pointer around arbitrarily (depositing a billion dollars in your account, or wiping you out), they face a regulator. If a game wants to wipe you out, well, you probably agreed to let them do that when you signed up.

Can you amass wealth in such a world? Well, sure. There are rich people in dictatorships all over the world. Stalin's favorites had great big dachas and drove fancy cars. You don't need democratic rights to get rich.

But you *do* need democratic freedoms to *stay* rich. In-world wealth is like a Stalin-era dacha, or the diamond fortunes of Apartheid South Africa: valuable, even portable (to a limited extent), but not really *yours*, not in any stable, long-term sense.

Here are some examples of the difference between being a citizen and a customer:

In January 2006, a World of Warcraft moderator shut down an advertisement for a "GBLT-friendly" guild. This was a virtual club that players could join, whose mission was to be "friendly" to "Gay/Bi/Lesbian/Transgendered" players. The WoW moderator—and Blizzard management—cited a bizarre reason for the shut-down:

"While we appreciate and understand your point of view, we do feel that the advertisement of a 'GLBT friendly' guild is very likely to result in harassment for players that may not have existed otherwise. If you will look at our policy, you will notice the suggested penalty for violating the Sexual Orientation Harassment Policy is to 'be temporarily suspended from the game.' However, as there was clearly no malicious intent on your part, this penalty was reduced to a warning."

Sara Andrews, the guild's creator, made a stink and embarrassed Blizzard (the game's parent company) into reversing the decision.

The rules of virtual worlds are embodied in EULAs, not constitutions, and are always "subject to change without notice."

In 2004, a player in the MMO EVE Online declared that the game's creators had stacked the deck against him, called EVE "a poorly designed game which rewards the greedy and violent, and punishes the hardworking and honest." He was upset over a change in the game dynamics which made it easier to play a pirate and harder to play a merchant.

The player, "Dentara Rask," wrote those words in the preamble to a tell-all memoir detailing an elaborate Ponzi scheme that he and an accomplice had perpetrated in EVE. The two of them had bilked EVE's merchants out of a substantial fraction of the game's total GDP and then resigned their accounts. The objective was to punish the game's owners for their gameplay decisions by crashing the game's economy.

In both of these instances, players—residents of virtual worlds—resolved their conflicts with game management through customer activism. That works in the real world, too, but when it fails, we have the rule of law. We can sue. We can elect new leaders. When all else fails, we can withdraw all our money from the bank, sell our houses, and move to a different country.

But in virtual worlds, these recourses are off-limits. Virtual worlds can and do freeze players' wealth for "cheating" (amassing gold by exploiting loopholes in the system), for participating in real-world gold-for-cash exchanges (eBay recently put an end to this practice on its service), or for violating some other rule. The rules of virtual worlds are embodied in EULAs, not constitutions, and are always "subject to change without notice."

So what does it mean to be "rich" in Second Life? Sure, you can have a thriving virtual business in game, one that returns a healthy sum of cash every month. You can even protect your profits by regularly converting them to real money. But if you lose an argument with Second Life's parent company, your business vanishes. In other worlds, the only stable in-game wealth is the wealth you take out of the game. Your virtual capital investments are totally contingent. Anger the wrong exec at Linden Labs, Blizzard, Sony Online Entertainment, or Sularke and your little in-world business could disappear for good.

Well, what of it? Why not just create a "democratic" game that has a constitution, full citizenship for players, and all the prerequisites for stable wealth? Such a game would be open source (so that other, interoperable "nations" could be established for you to emigrate to if you don't like the will of the majority in one game-world), and run by elected representatives who would instruct the administrators and programmers as to how to run the virtual world. In the real world, the TSA sets the rules for aviation—in a virtual world, the equivalent agency would determine the physics of flight.

It's my sneaking suspicion that the only people who'd enjoy playing World of Democracycraft would be the people running for office there.

The question is, would this game be any *fun*? Well, democracy itself is pretty fun—where "fun" means "engrossing and engaging." Lots of people like to play the democracy game, whether by voting every four years or by moving to K Street and setting up a lobbying operation.

But video games aren't quite the same thing. Gameplay conventions like "grinding" (repeating a task), "leveling up" (attaining a higher level of accomplishment), "questing" and so on are functions of artificial scarcity. The difference between a character with 10,000,000 gold pieces and a giant, rare, terrifying crossbow and a newbie player is which pointers are associated with each character's database entry. If the elected representatives direct that every player should have the shiniest armor, best spaceships, and largest bank balances possible (this sounds like a pretty good election platform to me!), then what's left to do?

Oh sure, in Second Life they have an interesting crafting economy based on creating and exchanging virtual objects. But these objects are *also* artificially scarce—that is, the ability of these objects to propagate freely throughout the world is limited only by the software that supports them. It's basically the same economics of the music industry, but applied to every field of human endeavor in the entire (virtual) world.

Fun matters. Real-world currencies rise and fall based, in part, by the economic might of the nations that issue them. Virtual world currencies are more strongly tied to whether there's any reason to spend the virtual currency on the objects that are denominated in it. 10,000 EverQuest golds might trade for $100 on a day when that same sum will buy you a magic EQ sword that enables you to play alongside the most interesting people online, running the most fun missions online. But if all those players out-migrate to World of Warcraft, and word gets around that Warlord's Command is way more fun than anything in poor old creaky EverQuest, your EverQuest gold turns into Weimar Deutschemarks, a devalued currency that you can't even give away.

This is where the plausibility of my democratic, cooperative, open source virtual world starts to break down. Elected governments can field armies, run schools, provide health care (I'm a Canadian), and bring acid lakes back to health. But I've never done anything run by a government agency that was a lot of *fun*. It's my sneaking suspicion that the only people who'd enjoy playing World of Democracycraft would be the people running for office. . . .

And hell, maybe bureaucracies have hidden reserves of fun that have been lurking there, waiting for the chance to bust out and surprise us all.

I sure hope so. These online worlds are endlessly diverting places. It'd be a shame if it turned out that cyberspace was a dictatorship—benevolent or otherwise.

Organizations to Contact

The editors have compiled the following list of organizations concerned with the issues debated in this book. The descriptions are derived from materials provided by the organizations. All have publications or information available for interested readers. The list was compiled on the date of publication of the present volume; the information provided here may change. Be aware that many organizations take several weeks or longer to respond to inquiries, so allow as much time as possible.

Digital Games Research Association
33014 University of Tampere
  Finland
e-mail: coordinator@digra.org
Web site: www.digra.org

The Digital Games Research Association (DiGRA) is an international association for academics and professionals who research digital games and related phenomena. DIGRA publishes columns and a digital library of research papers by members on its Web site.

Entertainment Software Association
575 Seventh Street, NW, Suite 300, Washington, DC 20004
(202) 223-2400
e-mail: esa@theesa.com
Web site: www.theesa.com

The Entertainment Software Association (ESA) is a U.S. association dedicated to serving the business and public affairs needs of companies that publish video and computer games for video game consoles, personal computers, and the Internet. The ESA offers a range of services to its members, including operating a global anti-piracy program, staging the annual Electronic Entertainment Expo gaming convention, fielding business and consumer research, and representing the industry at the federal, state, and local levels on a wide range of policy issues. It publishes fact sheets and compilations of research findings and commentaries on important industry issues, particularly the relationship between games and violence.

Federation of American Scientists
1717 K Street, NW, Suite 209, Washington, DC   20036
(202) 546-3300 • fax: (202) 675-1010
Web site: www.fas.org

The Federation of American Scientists (FAS) was formed in 1945 by atomic scientists from the Manhattan Project to promote humanitarian uses of science and technology. The FAS Information Technologies Project works on strategies to harness the potential of emerging information technologies to improve teaching and learning. In addition to producing several educational games, this group publishes a variety of reports, including 2006's "Harnessing the Power of Video Games for Learning."

International Game Developers' Association
19 Mantua Road, Mount Royal, NJ   08061
(856) 423-2990 • fax: (856) 423-3420
e-mail: contact@igda.org
Web site: www.igda.org

The International Game Developers' Association (IGDA) is made up of those involved with and interested in the development of digital games. The IGDA is committed to advancing the careers and enhancing the lives of game developers by connecting members with their peers, promoting professional development, and advocating on issues that affect the developer community. Its Web site offers papers, articles, and a newsletter on topics of interest to professional game developers, for example, quality of life, diversity, and anti-censorship.

John D. and Catherine T. MacArthur Foundation
140 South Dearborn Street, Chicago, IL   60603-5285
(312) 726-8000 • fax: (312) 920-6258

e-mail: 4answers@macfound.org
Web site: www.digitallearning.macfound.org

The John D. and Catherine T. MacArthur Foundation is a private grantmaking institution dedicated to fostering improvement in the human condition. In 2006, the Foundation launched a $50 million digital media and learning initiative to help determine how digital technologies are changing the way young people learn, play, socialize, and participate in civic life. In 2007, it explored how to help advance the use of virtual worlds for social benefit. Research reports, news, and youth testimonials from these projects are published regularly on the Foundation's Web site.

National Institute on Media and the Family
606 Twenty-fourth Avenue S, Suite 606
Minneapolis, MN   55454
(612) 672-5437 • fax: (612) 672-4113
Web site: www.mediafamily.org

The National Institute on Media and the Family is a conservative, research-based organization focused on the positive and harmful effects of media, including television, the Internet, and video games. The organization provides research, training materials, speakers, and consultancy to help create media choices for families, so that the United States has healthier, less violent communities. Publications available on the Institute's Web site include reports, columns, brochures, and fact sheets on video games.

New Media Consortium
2499 South Capital of Texas Highway, Building A, Suite 202
Austin, TX   78746-7762
(512) 445-4200 • fax: (512) 445-4205
e-mail: info@nmc.org
Web site: www.nmc.org

The New Media Consortium (NMC) is a community of hundreds of leading universities, colleges, museums, and research centers. The NMC stimulates and advances the exploration and use of new media and technologies for learning and creative expression. It publishes newsletters and research reports, such as the annual *Horizon Report*, on developments in educational technologies; its NMC Virtual Worlds Project helps educators and learning-focused organizations to explore, build, or establish a presence in a range of virtual worlds.

On-Line Gamers Anonymous

P.O. Box 5646, Harrisburg, PA   17110
(612) 245-1115
e-mail: olga@olganon.org
Web site: www.olganon.org

On-Line Gamers Anonymous is dedicated to helping those addicted to computer/video/console/online games and their friends and families. It provides a twelve-step program for recovery and healing from excessive game-playing based on the Alcoholics Anonymous model. The Web site provides discussion forums for organization members and visitors, as well as relevant articles and suggested readings that can be accessed free.

Bibliography

Books

Thor Alexander, ed. *Massively Multiplayer Game Development 2*. Hingham, MA: Charles River Media, 2005.

Craig A. Anderson, Douglas A. Gentile, and Katherine E. Buckley *Violent Video Game Effects on Children and Adolescents: Theory, Research, and Public Policy*. New York: Oxford University Press, 2007.

Jack M. Balkin and Beth Simone Noveck, eds. *The State of Play: Law, Games, and Virtual Worlds*. New York: New York University Press, 2006.

Richard A. Bartle *Designing Virtual Worlds*. Indianapolis, IN: New Riders Publishing, 2004.

John C. Beck and Mitchell Wade *Got Game: How the Gamer Generation Is Reshaping Business Forever*. Boston, MA: Harvard Business School Press, 2004.

David Bell, Brian D. Loader, Nicholas Pleace and Douglas Schuler, eds. *Cyberculture: The Key Concepts*. New York: Routledge, 2004.

Brenda Brathwaite *Sex in Video Games*. Boston, MA: Charles River Media, 2007.

Paul Carr and Graham Pond	*The Unofficial Tourists' Guide to Second Life.* New York: St. Martin's Press, 2007.
Edward Castronova	*Exodus to the Virtual World: How Online Fun Is Changing Reality.* New York: Palgrave Macmillan, 2007.
Heather Chaplin and Aaron Ruby	*Smartbomb: The Quest for Art, Entertainment, and Big Bucks in the Videogame Revolution.* Chapel Hill, NC: Algonquin Books, 2005.
Robbie Cooper, Julian Dibbell, and Tracy Spaight	*Alter Ego: Avatars and Their Creators.* London, U.K.: Chris Boot, 2007.
Julian Dibbell	*Play Money: Or, How I Quit My Day Job and Made Millions Trading Virtual Loot.* New York: Basic Books, 2006.
James Paul Gee	*What Video Games Have to Teach Us About Learning and Literacy.* New York: Palgrave Macmillan, 2003.
Henry Jenkins	*Fans, Bloggers, and Gamers: Exploring Participatory Culture.* New York: New York University Press, 2006.
Steven Johnson	*Everything Bad Is Good for You: How Today's Popular Culture Is Actually Making Us Smarter.* New York: Riverhead Books, 2005.
R. V. Kelly II	*Massively Multiplayer Online Role-Playing Games: The People, the Addiction and the Playing Experience.* Jefferson, NC: McFarland, 2004.

Brad King and John Borland	*Dungeons and Dreamers: The Rise of Computer Game Culture from Geek to Chic.* Emeryville, CA: McGraw-Hill/ Osborne, 2003.
Raph Koster	*A Theory of Fun for Game Design.* Scottsdale, AZ: Paraglyph Press, 2005.
David Kushner	*Masters of Doom: How Two Guys Created an Empire and Transformed Pop Culture.* New York: Random House, 2003.
Marc Prensky	*"Don't Bother Me Mom, I'm Learning!": How Computer and Video Games Are Preparing Your Kids for Twenty-First Century Success and How You Can Help.* St. Paul, MN: Paragon House, 2006.
Joost Raessens and Jeffrey Goldstein, eds.	*Handbook of Computer Game Studies.* Cambridge, MA: MIT Press, 2005.
Michael Rymaszewski, et al.	*Second Life: The Official Guide.* Indianapolis, IN: Wiley Publishing, 2007.
Ralph Schroeder and Ann-Sofie Axelsson, eds.	*Avatars at Work and Play: Collaboration and Interaction in Shared Virtual Environments.* Dordrecht, Netherlands: Springer, 2006.
David Williamson Shaffer	*How Computer Games Help Children Learn.* New York: Palgrave Macmillan, 2006.
John Suler	*The Psychology of Cyberspace*, revised version, 2007. www-usr.rider.edu/ ˜suler/psycyber/psycyber.html.

Mark J. P. Wolf and Bernard Perron, eds. *The Video Game Theory Reader.* New York: Routledge, 2003.

Periodicals

Susan Arendt "Doctor Urges AMA to Recognize Game Addiction as a Disorder," *Wired*, June 14, 2007.

Alicia Ault "Turn On, Tune Out, Get Well?" *Washington Post*, October 4, 2005.

Jack Balkin "Virtual Liberty: Freedom to Design and Freedom to Play in Virtual Worlds," *Virginia Law Review*, 2005.

Celeste Biever "The Irresistible Rise of Cybersex: From Full-on Encounters to Online Dating with a Twist, Simulated Sex is on the Up in Mainstream Gaming," *New Scientist*, June 17, 2006.

Kyle Brazzel "Multiplayer Mania: In Some Circles, Tragic Headlines Have Sparked Alarms About 'Addiction' to Online Video Games," *Arkansas Democrat-Gazette*, March 28, 2007.

Leslie Brody "Can You Be a Video-Game 'Addict'?" *Seattle Times*, August 19, 2006.

John Seely Brown and Douglas Thomas "You Play World of Warcraft? You're Hired!" *Wired*, April 1, 2006.

Business Wire	"Gartner Says 80 Percent of Active Internet Users Will Have a 'Second Life' in the Virtual World by the End of 2011," April 24, 2007.
Edward Castronova	"On Virtual Economies," *Game Studies*, December 2003.
Marcus D. Childress and Ray Braswell	"Using Massively Multiplayer Online Role-Playing Games for Online Learning," *Distance Education*, August 2006.
Current Events	"Living a Second Life: Virtual Worlds Create New Reality," January 22, 2007.
Sara de Freitas and Mark Griffiths	"Online Gaming as an Educational Tool in Learning and Training," *British Journal of Educational Technology*, June 2007.
Julian Dibbell	"The Unreal Estate Boom," *Wired*, January 1, 2003.
Economist	"A Model Economy," January 22, 2005.
Economist	"Breeding Evil? The Real Impact of Video Games," August 6, 2005.
Anthony Faiola	"When Escape Seems Just a Mouse-Click Away: Stress-Driven Addiction to Online Games Spikes in South Korea," *Washington Post*, May 27, 2006.
Allison Fass	"Sex, Pranks, and Reality," *Forbes*, February 7, 2007.

Alison George   "Striking Out for the New Territory," *New Scientist*, October 21, 2006.

Mark D. Griffiths, Mark N. O. Davies, and Darren Chappell   "Breaking the Stereotype: The Case of Online Gaming," *CyberPsychology & Behavior*, November 2003.

Cathy Lynn Grossman   "Net Faithful Find Second Life," *USA Today*, April 2, 2007.

Paul Ryan Hiebert   "Games for People Who Want to Change the World," *Canadian Dimension*, November–December 2006.

Becky Hogge   "Virtually the Same as Normal: Many Are Turning to Second Life Just as It Starts to Mirror the Real World," *New Statesman*, October 30, 2006.

Moon Ihlwan   "South Korea: Video Games' Crazed Capital," *Business Week*, March 26, 2007.

James D. Ivory   "Still a Man's Game: Gender Representation in Online Reviews of Video Games," *Mass Communication and Society*, Winter 2006.

David R. Johnson   "How Online Games May Change the Law and Legally Significant Institutions," *New York Law School Review*, 2004–2005.

F. Gregory Lastowka and Dan Hunter   "The Laws of the Virtual Worlds," University of Pennsylvania Law School Public Law and Legal Theory Research Paper Series, May 2003.

Carrie Levine   "Schools, Libraries Finding Second
                     Life in Second Life: Groups Test Wa-
                     ters of Online 'Metaverse,'" *Charlotte
                     Observer*, February 10, 2007.

Steven Levy, et al. "Living a Virtual Life," *Newsweek*,
                     September 18, 2006.

David Lipke   "Big Game Hunters," *Daily News
                     Record*, February 12, 2007.

Regina Lynn   "Second Life Gets Sexier," *Wired*, Au-
                     gust 25, 2006.

Michel Marriott   "We Have to Operate, but Let's Play
                     First," *New York Times*, February 24,
                     2005.

PC Advisor Staff   "Three Minutes With: Second Life
                     Exec," *PC World*, April 21, 2007.

lvars Peterson   "Games Theory: Online Play Can
                     Help Researchers Tackle Tough Com-
                     putational Problems," *Science News*,
                     March 17, 2007.

Jonathan Rauch   "Sex, Lies, and Video Games," *Atlan-
                     tic Monthly*, November 2006.

Cynthia Reynolds   "Videogame Widows," *Maclean's*,
                     January 16, 2006.

Bonnie Ruberg   "Sex in Games: It's a Turn-On,"
                     Wired, June 13, 2006.

Richard Siklos   "A Virtual World but Real Money,"
                     New York Times, October 19, 2006.

Mike Snider
"Video Games Actually Can Be Good for You," *USA Today*, September 27, 2005.

Joel Stein
"My So-Called Second Life," *Time*, December 16, 2006.

Kurt Squire and Constance Steinkuehler
"Meet the Gamers: They Research, Teach, Learn, and Collaborate. So Far, Without Libraries," *Library Journal*, April 2005.

Chris Suellentrop
"Playing with Our Minds," *Wilson Quarterly*, Summer 2006.

Aimee Tompkins
"The Psychological Effects of Violent Media on Children," *AllPsych Journal*, December 14, 2003.

Monica T. Whitty
"Pushing the Wrong Buttons: Men's and Women's Attitudes Toward Online and Offline Infidelity," *CyberPsychology and Behavior*, December 2003.

Dmitri Williams
"Excessive Online Gaming," *Washington Post*, August 18, 2006.

Dmitri Williams
"Groups and Goblins: The Social and Civic Impact of an Online Game," *Journal of Broadcasting & Electronic Media*, December 2006.

Dmitri Williams and Marko Skoric
"Internet Fantasy Violence: A Test of Aggression in an Online Game," *Communication Monographs*, June 2005.

| Wylie Wong | "Gaming in Education," *EdTech*, May–June 2007. |
| Nick Yee | "The Labor of Fun," *Games and Culture*, January 2006. |

Internet Resources

| Andrea Lynn | "No Strong Link Seen Between Violent Video Games and Aggression," www.physorg.com, August 11, 2005. |
| Grace Wong | "Educators Explore 'Second Life' Online," www.cnn.com, November 14, 2006. |

Web Sites

The Daedalus Project Web site: www.nickyee.com/daedalus. The Daedalus Project is an ongoing study of the psychology of more than 40,000 MMORPG players directed by Stanford University researcher Nick Yee, an expert on online games and immersive virtual reality. An extensive library of Yee's reports on the results of his research and a lexicon of MMORPG terms and abbreviations are available at this site.

GameDev.net Web site: www.gamedev.net. GameDev.net claims to be the leading online community for game developers of all levels, from beginners to industry veterans. According to its published numbers, over 350,000 developers from around the world take advantage of the frequently updated developer news, thousands of articles and tutorials, and active forums on its Web site.

MMOGChart.com Web site: www.mmogchart.com. This Web site provides an ongoing, unbiased analysis of the numbers of people participating in MMOGs. Site author

Bruce Sterling Woodcock is an independent MMOG consultant who has been active with MUDs and a variety of other online communities since the early 1990s. The Web site provides detailed reports and charts that describe and illustrate Woodcock's research into MMOG subscription numbers and growth rates worldwide.

Terra Nova Web site: http://terranova.blogs.com. Terra Nova is a Web log that offers news and many contributors' opinions regarding the social, economic, legal, psychological, and political aspects of virtual worlds.

Index